FINDING PEACE IN THE MIDST OF CHAOS

BY TERRI CRUZE

Copyright © 2005
Created in Christ, Publishing Division
www.cicpublishing.org

All rights reserved. No part of this book may be reproduced in any form, except for the inclusion of brief quotations in a review, without permission in writing from the author or publisher.

Library of Congress Card Number: 2005938415

ISBN 0-9711051-1-1

Created in Christ, Publishing Division
P.O. Box 391973
Snellville, Ga. 30039

Printed in the U.S.A. by
Lightning Source, Inc.
A Subsidiary of Ingram Industries Inc.
1246 Heil Quaker Blvd.
La Vergne, TN. USA 37086

Scripture references used in this book are from the following sources:

The King James Version of the Bible (KJV).

Holy Bible, New International Version (R), (NIV).
copyright, (c) 1973, 1978, 1984 by International Bible society.
Used by permission of Zondervan. All rights reserved.

New King James Version (R), (NKJV)
copyright, (c) 1982, Thomas Nelson, Inc., Nashville, Tennessee.
Used by permission. All rights reserved.

Holy Bible, New Living Translation, (NLT)
copyright, (c) 1996. Used by permission of Tyndale House Publishers, Inc.,
Wheaton, Illinois 60189. All rights reserved.

TABLE OF CONTENTS

Introduction i

Chapter 1:   We Are Called To Forgive 1

Chapter 2:   Forgiving Our Enemies 11

Chapter 3:   Forgiving and Forgetting 18

Chapter 4:   What Peace Is Not 25

Chapter 5:   What Is Peace? 34

Chapter 6:   A Sabbath Rest 42

Chapter 7:   Contentment 49

Chapter 8:   Attitude of Gratitude 58

Chapter 9:   Peace In God's Word 68

Chapter 10: Spiritual Warfare 77

Appendix 1: Discussion Questions 87

INTRODUCTION

Ah, chaos! A perfect description of what life is like on planet earth. Doesn't it sometimes feel like life is just one big problem after another? As a mother of three busy teenagers, working a more-than-full-time job as a nurse and juggling the overwhelming duties of my career and my responsibilities as a wife and a parent, I understand the pressures of daily life. There simply isn't enough time in a day to do all of the things I feel I need to do in the way they ought to be done, or at least to measure up to my own unrealistic standards. I pressure myself to be the perfect wife, mother, friend, coworker, supervisor, patient advocate, citizen, and Christian, none of which is truly possible. And these are just my "normal" days. Then there are the added struggles of illnesses, job changes, family conflicts, and other issues. For me, it is as though I just make it through one crisis, only to be faced with another. Then, when things start to calm down, it is tough to enjoy myself, because I just know another catastrophe is waiting for me around the next corner. Or at least, that's how I used to feel. If this scenario strikes a familiar chord in your life, read on. There really is help.

The Lord has been very patient with me. He has led me through many trials in an effort to improve my character. But these character-building exercises have been difficult at best, and have often led me to question God's motives and my ability to follow Him. Many times, I have asked for peace, only to face more turmoil. I couldn't understand, at first, why my pleas for mercy and peace would be met with challenges and trials. I felt I was being punished; that somehow I wasn't good enough, or my faith wasn't strong enough for me to be worthy of God's blessings.

Thankfully, God enlightened me, showing me that it wasn't about being worthy; it was about His gift of grace. He taught me about His will for my life and His overall plan to give me victory. I finally understood the meaning of peace and how to attain it. It is my prayer that as you read of my experiences and glean wisdom from God's word, that you will find the source of peace that I have found.

I pray that as you explore God's word, you will discover the path toward peace and gain fresh insight into God's plans for developing your character, so that you can be outfitted for eternity with Him. Please journey with me on a road that will lead us into a deeper relationship with Christ and a more complete understanding of His will. I make no apology for my heavy reliance on scripture in this book, as this is the tool God gives us to help us understand His will for our lives. Through my experiences and my relationship with Christ, I have been moved to write this book, in order to bring healing to someone else who may be struggling with similar issues. If you have been yearning for a deeper relationship with Christ, for healing of unyielding pain, for forgiveness of secret sins that keep haunting your soul, please join me in opening your heart to God where this healing begins.

God is reaching out to you, personally inviting you to follow his plan for your life. Take the time to respond to His call. Listen to His counsel, learn from the examples in His word, and take hold of the grace He freely offers to each of us that hears His voice and follows Him.

In this book you will explore God's forgiveness toward us as sinners, examine your responsibility in forgiving others, and ultimately discover the tools you can use to obtain the peace that He offers to our burdened souls. He offers it freely; He wants us to have it. "If you then, being evil, know how to give good gifts to your children, how much more will your Father who is in heaven give good things to those who ask Him" (Matt 7:11, NKJV). So, let's begin.

WE ARE CALLED TO FORGIVE

The biggest obstacles on my own path toward peace have been resentment and anger. The first step I had to take was to learn to forgive those in my life that had caused me pain. Unresolved conflicts tend to grow and fester, robbing us of the peace we desperately need. It is essential that we learn to forgive our friends, Our families, ourselves, and even our enemies, if we are to experience God's peace in our lives.

The Bible tells us clearly that forgiveness is at the heart of peace. For example, Proverbs 19:11 states: "A man's wisdom gives him patience; it is to his glory to overlook an offense" (NIV). We are encouraged to patiently "overlook" wrongs done to us in order to have peace. How can we have peace if we are carrying a grudge or if we are quick to become angry over every little thing that doesn't go our way?

For many years, my resentment and anger toward my parents kept me from being at peace. My father and mother divorced when I was very young. My mother told me that their marriage had failed because she became pregnant with me, and children were not part of my father's plans. Throughout my childhood, I had felt unloved and abandoned by my father and guilty about ruining their marriage.

My mother remarried soon after the divorce. My step-father, who adopted me, was a very abusive man, both physically and sexually. My mother was quite aware of the abuse, but she did nothing to stop it from continuing. I was angry at my father for giving me away to this "monster". I was even angrier at my step-father for all of the abuse, and I found it impossible to accept that my mother could love me, while she allowed me to be treated so terribly.

As I had no positive outlet for all of this anger, I turned it on myself. I starved myself and became obsessed with losing weight. That didn't help. I turned to alcohol, but found no cure for the pain. One desperate night, I even attempted suicide, but thankfully, my attempt was unsuccessful. (A fellow student in after-school detention had shared with me some advice on how to do it more efficiently. Praise God, she was wrong!) I found no escape.

It was after this that I found the only true solution to my problems, the only cure for my pain. I left home and moved in with a friend, whose Christian family provided an oasis of love and support. I began attending church regularly and had an opportunity to see how a "normal" family worked. I learned about a God that cared about me personally and found a love I had never known. I continue to thank God for this precious experience, because this would help me to survive the hardships that were yet to come.

My mother convinced me to move back home after a few months. I finally agreed, as she promised that things would be different. I desperately wanted to believe her. But, things were no different. Then, along came my knight in shining armor.

I was sixteen at the time, and I met a man, through a neighbor that I babysat for. He was twenty-four and was quite a charmer! He swept me off my feet. He told me how much he loved me, he promised to provide for me and protect me, and he asked me to marry him. He was everything I had dreamed of. We were married when I was seventeen.

It was far from a match made in heaven. The mother of the family that I had lived with begged me not to go through with the wedding. My aunt and my grandmother tried to discourage me; they knew I was in for heartache and suffering, but I wouldn't listen. What did these "old people" know, anyway? I was determined to prove them all wrong. But, I couldn't.

My husband was more of a monster than my step-dad was. He was heavy into the drug scene. He would take off for days at a time, then come home and accuse me of cheating on him. He verbally abused me. He beat me. One time, he forced me to have sex with him at gunpoint. He even tried to kill me. I sent him to jail once for assault. When he got out, he told me he had learned his lesson: he "would not leave any marks the next time."

Then my mother died. It tore my world apart! I would never have the chance to make things right with her. I became aware of my own mortality. Everything changed. I left my husband, filed for divorce, became a vegetarian, (so I wouldn't die young, too), and I fully surrendered my heart to God. Meanwhile, my husband didn't enjoy life on his own, so he decided to go to drug rehab. I chose to give him another chance, and I did not go through with the divorce. We conceived our second child during this reconciliation. Things were finally coming together.

For two years, life was great. Then it all started again: the drugs, the abuse, the paranoia. It got so bad that I feared for my life every day. I was certain that one day I would come home, and he would be waiting for me. I feared he would kill us all and then himself. Praise God, it did not happen that way. Instead, things took a turn on the day after Thanksgiving. My husband was really strung out on drugs and was once again making accusations about my fidelity. He told me that if I didn't tell him the truth, he would leave me. There was nothing to tell, but he didn't believe me. He left that night. The next day, he came back while I was at church and emptied out the house. This was my ticket out! I changed the locks, filed for divorce, filed a restraining order against him, and finally started to move forward toward a new life.

He came back several times to ask me to do his laundry, loan him some money, etc. Finally he realized it was over. But then tragedy struck. Less than a month after our divorce was final, he committed suicide. This was made even more difficult, as his family blamed me for not being there for him and preventing it somehow.

So, by the age of 26, I had experienced much heartache and tragedy. I had much to forgive and to be forgiven for. Luckily, God doesn't expect us to heal overnight, and He is patient, willing, and able to show us the way through the pain and into His peace. I have found much comfort in the consistency of God's word regarding forgiveness.

For instance, Jesus, when teaching his disciples how to pray made a point about the importance of forgiveness:

"Pray like this: Our Father in heaven may your name be honored. May your Kingdom come soon. May your will be done here on earth, just as it is in heaven. Give us our food for today, and forgive us our sins, just as we have forgiven those who have sinned against us. And don't let us yield to temptation, but deliver us from the evil one. If you forgive those who sin against you, your heavenly Father will forgive you. But if you refuse to forgive others, your Father will not forgive your sins" (Matthew 6:9-15, NLT).

Here, we have a very clear command to practice forgiveness, and we are given an idea of how important it is to God that we put this into action. Once more, Mark 11:25, 26 tells us: "And whenever you stand praying, if you have anything against anyone, forgive him, that your Father in heaven may also forgive you your trespasses. But if you do not forgive, neither will your Father in heaven forgive your trespasses." (NKJV). Also: "Therefore if you bring your gift to the altar, and there remember that your brother has something against you, leave your gift there before the altar, and go your way. First be reconciled to your brother, and then come and offer your gift" (Matthew 5:23, 24, NKJV).

God wishes us to have peace in our relationships, and wants us to make this a priority. That is why He would tell us to leave our gift at the altar and make things right with our "brother" first. God will be there for us always. Our gift to him can wait. How can he accept our offering if we are not right with our families and friends? We cannot come to Him with a prayerful heart, ready to follow where He leads us, ready for cleansing and healing, if we are still engaged in a conflict with someone close to us. He wants our whole heart, not just the part we are willing to give. God is a god of love, and He needs us to reflect that love in all of our relationships, if we are to be called His children.

Another point the Bible teaches us about forgiveness is found in 2 Corinthians 2:7. We are told that when someone causes us grief, we should "…forgive and comfort him, so that he will not be overwhelmed by excessive sorrow." (NIV). We must, as Christians, consider the needs and ultimate salvation of even those who do us wrong. We cannot know what lessons God may have in store for that person, and how our response may ultimately shape his experience, or lead him in his walk with God.

Once again, we are reminded of the link between forgiveness and peace in Colossians 3:12-15:

> *"Therefore, as the elect of God, holy and beloved, put on tender mercies, kindness, humility, meekness, longsuffering; bearing with one another, and forgiving one another, if anyone has a complaint against another; even as Christ forgave you, so you also must do. But above all these things put on love, which is the bond of perfection. And let the peace of*

God rule in your hearts, to which also you were called in one body; and be thankful." (NKJV).

This verse clearly shows that a loving, forgiving character is needed in order to obtain the peace we are seeking. Again, we are reminded that we must be like Christ, loving and willing to forgive, if we wish to have peace in our hearts.

So, all of this sounds great, in theory, right? But what about the application? How are we supposed to actually live it out in our own lives? Forgiveness is hard work! Is God telling us to back down and give in every time we are in a conflict? Well, don't despair! God gives us the answers to these difficult questions as well.

First of all, the Bible is full of examples of the way He forgives and how He expects us to forgive. He shows us what happens if we choose to let anger and hatred reign in our hearts as well as examples of what can happen if we can move beyond our pain and reach out to those who have hurt us, with love and compassion. There are too many examples to discuss in this book, but I would like to explore a few, to get us started.

The first example to come to mind is the story of the prodigal, or lost, son. You can find it in Luke 15:11-32. Here we find a story of a young man who asks his father for his inheritance early, so he can run off into the world to find his own way. I can certainly relate to this young man, as I, too, tried to make a new life for myself, away from the influences of my parents. He seems like a typical teen, thinking he knows more than the "old man" and wanting to prove himself to the world, to live by his own rules, instead of the "old-fashioned" ways of his "out-of-touch" parents. But he is ill-prepared for the realities of life on his own. He has a great time, partying, making friends, doing "his own thing," until (surprise!) he runs out of money. He then realizes that life isn't all about fun and games. He has to get a job and earn a living, or he will starve! Now, he remembers the good old days, at home, with Dad, a warm bed, plenty of food, even servants that worked for him. He is certain that he blew it with his dad, but he decides that if he goes home and apologizes, maybe his dad will hire him on to work the family farm. Even his father's servants are better off than he is right now.

So, the young man returns home. "...But while he was still a long way off, his father saw him and was filled with compassion for him; he ran to his son, threw his arms around him and kissed him" (Luke 15:20, NIV). What a story of forgiveness! His son had wasted everything, had insulted his father by asking for what was not even rightly his at that time, and hadn't contacted his family since he left, to let them know if he was even alive. But the father wasn't worried about past hurts; his son had returned! He had been waiting and watching for him the whole time! This is just like the way our Father in heaven waits for us, when we are wayward children!

The story, however, does not end here. There is another son. This son also reminds me of my own actions. This son is not as good at forgiveness as his father. He is angry and jealous. Why should his father be so happy for his brother who had wasted everything, when he had stayed home and worked and had been so faithful to his father? Was his hard work to be ignored? Is that fair? His father has to acknowledge his faithfulness and remind him that his place is secure, before he will allow himself to celebrate his brother's return with his father. His father has to spell it out for him, so he can see past his own selfish desires. How often do we let anger and jealousy get in the way of our own happiness? I know I am guilty of this all too often. It takes a lot of practice to be able to move past our own selfishness to forgive others whom we feel may have an unfair advantage over us. But we have to do it, or the anger and jealousy will grow and fester, and will certainly stand in the way of any peace we might otherwise have.

I was able to learn to forgive my father for leaving me, not only by getting to know him and asking him about what happened (every story has more than one side), but also by allowing the Holy Spirit time to work on my own heart. Luckily, my father was truly sorry for the way things turned out, and he has worked hard to grow and nurture a relationship with me in my adult life. Learning that I was not the cause of my parents' divorce and that I was loved helped immensely to ease my pain. Forgiving him allowed me to grow emotionally and spiritually. I felt God at work in my heart.

Another story that has a great lesson for us is found in Matthew 18:21-35, called the parable of the unmerciful servant. Here, we have a story about a king that forgives a servant of a great deal of debt, a debt that he was unable to even begin to pay. The king could have sold not only the servant's belongings, but his family and the servant, himself, into slavery to begin to pay the debt, but the king chose to forgive the debt and let the servant go instead. This same servant then went out and found another man who owed him some money and violently threatened him and had him thrown into prison until he could repay the debt, which, of course, would be nearly impossible to do from prison! When the king heard about it, he could not believe that the servant who had been forgiven so much could do such a thing, instead of passing on the forgiveness that he was granted and extending it to the man who owed him such a small amount. The king had this man tortured until he could repay his debt, because of his unwillingness to show mercy to his fellow man. Jesus said this is an example of how the Father will respond to us, unless we are willing to practice forgiveness.

Think about it for a moment. Is there anything in your life, in my life, that God has had to forgive us for? I couldn't begin to count them all, can you? If God is so willing to forgive every single sin in our lives, from the greatest sin to even the smallest hidden thought, shouldn't we feel obligated to practice the same toward others? If we cannot forgive someone else for their own benefit, can we at least do it to show our gratitude to the Father for His grace and mercy toward us? Try it out. See for yourself.

Consider two examples from the life of Christ; after all, He is our ultimate example, the pattern we are to follow. Read Luke 7:36-50. Jesus was invited to the home of one of the Pharisees for dinner. An uninvited, "immoral" woman had heard that Jesus was there, so she came to Him and knelt at His feet, weeping. She began to dry her tears from His feet with her hair, while kissing them and pouring an entire jar of very expensive perfume on them. The Pharisee was completely offended by the presence of this sinful woman in his home, as well as the fact that Jesus would allow her to treat him that way. Did He not know who she was? Jesus read the man's thoughts and told him this parable:

> *"A man loaned money to two people—five hundred pieces of silver to one and fifty pieces to the other. But neither of them could repay him, so he kindly forgave them both, canceling their debts. Who do you suppose loved him more after that?"* (Luke 7:41, 42, NLT)

The Pharisee agreed that the one who had been forgiven the most loved the king the most. Jesus explained to him that the woman's kindness had even exceeded his own toward a guest in his home, by washing His feet, kissing Him, and anointing Him with perfume. Then He forgave her sins. The Pharisee and his other guests were angry and confused. How could this man, Jesus, have the power to forgive sins? Jesus did not respond to their questioning, but instead turned to the woman and said: "Your faith has saved you; go in peace" (Luke 7:50, NIV). The woman could now have the peace she needed, as she had faith that God had forgiven her sins.

Jesus knew that this woman was not there to discuss politics, or to show herself superior to others. She had no other agenda than to meet Jesus and to open her heart to him. Her tears are all the evidence we need of her sincerity.

She knew her sinfulness. She knew her sorrows. And she knew the only place she could get true forgiveness and find peace: at the feet of Jesus. This is as true for us today as it was for her. The way to peace is through forgiveness of sins, and then only through repentance at the feet of Jesus. He knows our hearts, just as he knew hers. He feels our tears. He wants us to have peace. Our faith, too, can save us, just as it did this "sinful" woman thousands of years ago.

The ultimate example from the life of Christ, in my opinion, occurred at the crucifixion. You can read in Luke, chapter 23, all that the Lord had to endure during his last 24 hours on earth. As he hung on the cross, being teased, tormented, and mocked, He pleaded, "Father, forgive them, for they do not know what they do" (Luke 23:34, NKJV). As He was dying, his concern was for others, even those that were tormenting Him. He could have mocked them back, laughed at their arrogance and their ignorance, or revealed to them the future punishment they would have to endure for their unbelief, but He didn't. Talk about loving your enemies! Could any of us actually pray for forgiveness for those who were killing us? That is love! He would have endured all of that for even one sinner, for just you or just me. He still loves us that much! If He wanted to forgive his enemies, can you imagine how He longs to forgive you and me? He is just waiting for us to ask.

FORGIVING OUR ENEMIES

Now that we have begun to explore forgiveness, I think it is time to dig a little deeper. We may have very little difficulty forgiving those we love, those who are close to us, and those whose salvation we are concerned about, especially if they are genuinely sorry. But what about those who may have hurt us deeply, perhaps even purposely? How do we forgive someone that has not even acknowledged that they have hurt us, let alone asked us for forgiveness? Does God really mean it when He tells us to forgive our enemies?

Absolutely! Here is where the really hard work starts. When someone hurts us at the deepest level, it is our nature to feel angry and resentful. We may be vengeful and even hate this person. That is our carnal nature; that is the way we're "wired". God's way goes against the natural tendency of our heart, but it is the only way toward finding peace. Letting go of the hatred, resentment, and anger is the only way we can heal and develop a closer relationship with our savior.

I can assure you that having experienced the pain and worked through the steps to forgive my parents, my ex-husband, and even myself, I understand how difficult and painful, and at the same time liberating, this process of forgiveness is. I know that without forgiveness, I could never have developed a healthy self esteem or grown beyond my bitterness toward peace and happiness. It took much prayer, dedication, and hard work to learn what God has shown me, so that I could quit being a victim and become victorious instead. When I continued to feel angry and was full of hatred and resentment toward my family, it kept robbing me of inner peace and tranquility. I continued to be victimized by them until I was able to give the whole matter over to God to take care of and to allow Him to change my heart. In order to regain control of my own emotions, I had to learn to forgive them and release the pain to God.

I have learned that forgiveness is a great healer, and the benefit to the forgiver greatly exceeds the benefit to the forgiven. If someone has hurt us, especially if they have intentionally caused us pain, it may be of no benefit to them at all if we forgive them. More than likely, they could care less if we forgive them, especially if they are not sorry for what they have done. But the benefit for us is tremendous. When we let go of all of the anger and the pain, we can feel the blessings being showered down upon us, and we can grow in our relationship with God. We begin to feel good about ourselves; the person who has hurt us has no more power over us to cause us any more pain. That is the victory!

After I left home and was no longer subject to the tyranny of my step-father, I began to let go of the hatred I felt toward him. As time passed, and as I continued to work on forgiving him, I was able to talk to him on the phone without becoming angry and reopening old wounds just by hearing the sound of his voice. I had to keep reminding myself that he had no power over me, and that I had the option of hanging up if I felt the least bit threatened. Eventually, I could even visit with him in person without feeling like a frightened child in his presence. I knew that God was with me, and that I was a valuable person to Him, so it didn't matter anymore what my step-father thought about me. I could do nothing on my own, to bring about this change in my heart. I trusted God to heal me, and He did. I felt so free once I was no longer controlled by fear.

My step-father never once apologized, or even admitted that he had done anything wrong. I could not have waited for him to make the first move, or the opportunity would never have presented itself to start the healing process. God does not ask us to forgive someone only if they have acknowledged their sins against us. This does not have to be a condition of our forgiveness, unless we are planning to develop a deeper relationship with the person. I was not looking for relationship, I only needed healing and closure, so that I could grow in my own relationship with God and mature as an individual.

Christ made the first step in the reconciliation process between God and man, as well. He made the ultimate sacrifice for us, while we were still dead in our sins. As we begin to understand the sacrifice that Christ made for us and allow the love of Christ to grow in us, we will begin to feel less angry toward those that hurt us. Through the Holy Spirit, we will gain the victory and learn to let go of the hurt and to love ourselves through the pain. When we learn to trust the promises of God, He will give us the strength and ability to forgive others and to let go of the bitterness and resentment. This will help lead us into a relationship of love and of peace in Christ. God is able to give us all the strength and power we need to follow through, if only we will ask Him.

Furthermore, God wishes for us to live in peace. He does not want us to be vengeful and full of hatred. As the scriptures tell us:

"Do not repay anyone evil for evil. Be careful to do what is right in the eyes of everybody. If it is possible, as far as it depends on you, live at peace with everyone. Do not take revenge, my friends, but leave room for God's wrath, for it is written: 'it is mine to avenge; I will repay,' says the Lord. On the contrary: 'If your enemy is hungry, feed him; if he is thirsty, give him something to drink. In doing this, you will heap

burning coals on this head.' Do not be overcome by evil, but overcome evil with good" Romans 12:17-21 (NIV).

God asks us to put aside our carnal desires for revenge and to continue to do what is right, even if, in our judgment, the other person does not deserve it.

Isaiah 55:9 states: "For as the heavens are higher than the earth, so are My ways higher than your ways, and My thoughts than your thoughts," (NKJV). God has great plans for us, which we may not always be able to see or understand from our vantage point. We cannot always understand His ways, but if we follow where He leads us, it will become clear to us in time. Our job, then, is to follow with what understanding we do have, and to trust Him with the rest. Know that He has a plan and that He will always work to bring about all that is good for us as we seek to follow Him.

This is not to mean that God wants us to suffer in oppression or that somehow abuse can be construed as God's will. Abuse should not be tolerated. We have the responsibility to stand up for our rights. But we also need to look for the lessons God may have for us in any situation and try to learn from our experiences, as He leads us through them.

Forgiving our enemies does so much to heal our own hearts. It may truly benefit our enemies, as well, as they respond to the love that we show them. As we read in the story of the unforgiving debtor, in Matthew 18, Peter had questioned Jesus about forgiveness. He wondered if we should forgive someone up to seven times, as was the custom at the time. Jesus said, "No, seventy times seven." Obviously this is not to be taken literally, for who could keep track of such a number? It was meant to show him that we should not be concerned with keeping score. We should just continue to forgive as often as it is warranted. As a Christian, we should *live* forgiveness. That is what Christ did.

For example, look at how Jesus responded in his own life to his enemies. He had been betrayed, beaten, mocked, tested, spit upon, ridiculed, disrobed, and even given vinegar to quench his thirst as he hung on the cross, while the soldiers were arguing over his clothing. His response was "…Father, forgive them, for they do not know what they are doing.…" (Luke 23:34, NIV). Imagine, a Savior so loving as to forgive the very people that were torturing and killing Him! That is the God we serve! He knows our sorrows and the troubles we are facing. He knows our hurts and our pain. He has experienced more than we would ever want to have to endure. Yet, He forgave even the cruelest men for their offenses, because they simply did not understand the eternal consequences of their actions!

Could it be that when we are wrongly accused, treated unjustly, gossiped about, and lied to, that others simply do not understand what they are doing, or how their actions might affect us? Is it possible that we, at times, are guilty of this as well? Sometimes we need to work toward understanding our enemies' needs and point of view, to help us better figure out how to deal with them. We can forgive them more easily if we understand why they may be doing what they are doing, and in understanding, we can help them find a better course of action that would not cause anyone else pain.

The whole universe is watching how we, as Christians, respond to just such situations. "…we have been made a spectacle to the whole universe, to angels as well as to men" (1 Corinthians 4:9, NIV) We never know whose life we may touch, what lessons we may teach, just by our response when circumstances make things tough. It is quite possible that our experiences are meant not only to build our own character, but to help others on their journey as well. Our actions have unlimited consequences, both good and bad. It is imperative, then, that we learn to follow Christ's example and practice the type of forgiveness he not only asks of us, but portrayed so beautifully and completely in His own life. We must look beyond ourselves to see how our actions can help or hinder others' progress toward a deeper experience with Christ.

So, in order to really practice this kind of forgiveness, we must have faith to work against our natural tendencies, our in-born nature of "looking out for number one" and paying back evil for evil. We must allow Christ to work in us to change our hearts and allow us to be forgiving. We cannot do anything like this in our own strength. It won't work! But the good news is that Christ has already promised to give us the strength and power we need to be able to follow Him: "For God has not given us a spirit of fear and timidity, but of power, love, and self-discipline" (2 Timothy 1:7, NLT). He builds our characters to help us follow Him more closely, and he changes our hearts to better understand His will and His love for us.

1 Corinthians 10:13 tells us "No temptation has seized you except what is common to man. And God is faithful; he will not let you be tempted beyond what you can bear. But when you are tempted, he will also provide a way out so that you can stand up under it." (NIV). Read that again. What a powerful verse! It tells us that our problems, our "temptations" if you will, are the same problems that are common to everyone! How easy it is to think we are the only ones who have to struggle. Get it straight: everyone struggles! It is COMMON to man! This really became apparent to me when I began speaking with other women who have been victims of domestic violence or of child abuse. I found that I was definitely not unique! When I struggle with relationships, finances, work issues, or other issues, I find again that these are not uniquely my problems. The details may be different, but the overall problems are pretty much a normal part of everyone's life. That is why Christ tells us that our temptations are common. That is also why the Bible can tell us that "This high priest of ours understands our weaknesses, for he faced all of the same temptations we do, yet he did not sin" (Hebrews 4:15, NLT). What a testimony! Christ understands, because he has been there! He knows what it feels like to be hurt by someone He loves, to be mistreated, to be betrayed with a kiss. He has experienced more betrayal than any of us would ever want to have to endure. He gets it! When we ask Him for

the strength to make the right decisions, He knows what we need, because He remembers what it was like for him. That is sympathy beyond what any human can experience.

It also says He will not tempt you beyond what you can bear. What a relief! Unfortunately, He knows exactly how much you can bear, so He can push you to the limit, if need be. Not so encouraging, huh? But the next part is the kicker: He will provide a way out for us. So, when it feels like you just can't take anymore, it's okay. There is a way out, for God has promised it. Our job, then, is simply to pay attention and follow His lead. When we find that we are struggling to forgive, we need to remember that we have been provided with all that we need to make it happen. God will give us the power, the strength, and the way to do it. He will also be with us, cheering us on all the way! And it is worth the effort, when we finally experience His peace, instead of anger, hatred, pain, and frustration. Everyone has enemies to forgive. He is waiting right now. Are you ready to take that step of forgiveness?

FORGIVING AND FORGETTING

We have often heard the saying, "forgive and forget," but is that what God has asked us to do? How can we forget the powerful experiences that have shaped who we are and how we respond to the world around us? Does God ask us to forget, so that we can keep getting into the same problems with the same people over and over again? Does he want us to act like a doormat and tolerate abuse or allow others to take advantage of us? I would like to suggest that God certainly promises to forget our sins, but He has not asked us to do the same. While it would undoubtedly be easier to forgive if we could forget every bad thing that ever happens to us, would it really be beneficial? Let's explore this concept a little further.

The word "forget" is found several times in the Bible. Many of these texts record how God's people were told not to forget Him or their covenant with Him. In other verses, God assures His children that He would not forget His promises to them. There are also scriptures that teach us that God does not want us to forget our sins against Him. Likely, this is because it helps us to remember and focus on His saving grace and our need for the gift of mercy that He has given us. Also, in several places, the scripture records men of God asking Him not to forget them. Yet, I have not found even one verse asking us to forget the wrongs others have done against us, or those that we have committed against others. Forgive, certainly, but not forget.

While forgetting wrongs done against us may make it easier to forgive others, it would also keep us from gaining the wisdom of understanding God's grace. When we remember what has happened to us, and how we have overcome the temptation to hold grudges or harbor resentment, we are able to see God's development of our character. Even more, when we are aware of our own sins against God, and how far we have fallen, and we recognize what our sins have cost God, we are drawn to Him and can truly appreciate the sacrifice He has made for us. We become more grateful for His grace toward us. Our memory, therefore, was given to us to help us to learn and to grow.

I have learned to forgive my stepfather for abusing me as a child. I no longer hate him for what he has done. However, I do not let my daughters spend time alone with him or put them in a position where he could harm them. If I did not remember what had happened to me, I would not be able to protect my own children, or anyone else, from being hurt by this man.

Also, if I did not remember how I felt when I was young and my world was spinning so far out of control that I attempted suicide, I would not be able to choose a better course the next time I felt depressed or anxious about the future. I know through my experiences that God has rescued me before and has always been there to comfort me in my most difficult hours. If I am able to recall this when I go through struggles now, then I have hope, which renews my strength to persevere in my trials.

Just like everyone else, I have made mistakes in the past that have hurt my friends and my family. I know that no matter what I have done, God was able to make things better and to restore my relationship with Him and those I have hurt. By recalling those experiences and the ways in which God intervened, I have the assurance that no matter how badly I have messed up, God can still bring a blessing out of the trouble. That is how our trust grows in our relationship with God. We make a mess out of things, and God loves us anyway. He teaches us how to do it better the next time. We need our memory to learn from our mistakes and grow in our relationship with God and with each other.

Ezekiel 16:63 states: "Then, when I make atonement for you for all you have done, you will remember and be ashamed and never again open your mouth because of your humiliation, declares the Sovereign Lord" (NIV). Here, God appeals to our memory, to help us learn from our mistakes. Also, "There you will remember your conduct and all the actions by which you have defiled yourselves, and you will loathe yourselves for all the evil you have done" (Ezekiel 20:43, NIV). God gave us the ability to remember our sin, so that we will learn to hate it, as He does, and be driven to repent and to accept the salvation that He offers. Psalm 130:3, 4 states, "Lord, if you kept a record of our sins, who, O Lord, could ever survive? But you offer forgiveness, that we might learn to fear you" (NLT). Our memory is important in enhancing our learning. We are here, after all, to learn to live and to love like Christ. If we don't remember the lessons, how could we succeed? That being said, it is different with God:

"For my thoughts are not your thoughts, neither are your ways my ways,' declares the Lord. 'As the heavens are higher than the earth, so are my ways higher than your ways and my thoughts than your thoughts" (Isaiah 55: 8, 9, NIV).

He is able to forget, though not in the way we forget things. He is not absent-minded. He is able to remember, but he chooses to disregard the sins that we confess. Isaiah 43:25 states: "I, even I, am He who blots out your transgressions for My own sake; And I will not remember your sins" (NKJV). Note this is not for our benefit, but for His own sake! His forgiveness does more than assure us of our salvation. It professes His truth and establishes His character as a God of love to the whole universe. Again, in Jeremiah 31:34, we find: "...For I will forgive their wickedness and will remember their sins no more" (NIV). Also, "As far as the east is from the west, so far hath he removed our transgressions from us" (Psalm 103:12, KJV). He removes and separates our sin from us. God hates sin, but He loves us. He does not want to associate us with our sin. The New Testament confirms this: "Then he adds, 'I will never again remember their sins and lawless deeds" (Hebrews 10:17, NLT).

God wants us to know that His forgiveness is so complete that He will never bring our sins up again. He is not like us. When we argue with our spouses or our children, we often say things like, "You always do that. This is just like the time you..." We say we have forgiven them, but then we bring up the offense every time the person makes a mistake. With God, it is different. Micah 7:18, 19 states:

"Who is a God like you, who pardons sin and forgives the transgression of the remnant of his inheritance? You do not stay angry forever but delight to show mercy. You will again have compassion on us; you will tread our sins underfoot and hurl all our iniquities into the depths of the sea." (NIV).

God loves us so much that He chooses to cover all of our sins with the precious blood of Christ and to see only His love and mercy, rather than the shortcomings and wrongs of His people. Our job is simply to confess and allow Him to do the rest. "If we confess our sins, He is faithful and just to forgive us our sins and to cleanse us from all unrighteousness" (1 John 1:9, NKJV). He will faithfully forgive our sins, and will never again use them against us. They are covered with the blood of Christ, blotted out of his memory. They are truly "cleansed;" there is no more guilt or remorse for us to bear; we are free to come to him and grow in his grace.

How amazing it is that God chooses to forgive so completely! We can never again be fooled by the voice of our enemy, the devil, when he tries to convince us that we are not good enough! He cannot convince us that our sins will keep us from the peace that God offers us. God will never hold our sins against us, as long as we have repented and we have chosen to accept His forgiveness. While we may still have to face the consequences of our decisions and live with the results of our sins, we are free from the guilt of a sinful life, because God has set us free.

So, God's choice to banish our sins from His memory is a huge blessing for us. Without it, we could not experience salvation. But He does forgive us, and salvation can be ours. How could we hold back forgiveness from others, then, knowing how completely God has forgiven us? After all, He is our ultimate example. We are to follow Him, to think and to act like Him, to the best of our ability. Even though we cannot forget the sins of our adversaries, we should still make every effort to fully, completely forgive them. This would mean not bringing up old issues that have been resolved or prior wrongs that have been forgiven. We should act as though we have buried their sins, as God chooses to bury ours in the depth of the sea. This is truly following our Lord's example.

In that same manner, wouldn't it be great if we could practice that same forgiveness on ourselves? I don't know about you, but I cannot count the number of times I have remembered something I have done, or failed to do, that I wish I had done differently. There are times when I replay an event in my mind, trying to figure out why I made the choices I did, and having a very hard time forgiving myself. I am glad God is not as hard on me as I am on myself!

When my first husband committed suicide, I felt really guilty. It didn't help that some of his family members told me that if I had been there for him, he wouldn't have died. I asked myself over and over again, "What could I have done differently? How could I have helped him?" God helped me to see that I was not to blame. I could not have prevented his suicide any more than I could have caused it. So, I began to let go of the guilt and to forgive myself. I had to realize, once again, that I am not in control of the universe, and, therefore, I am not responsible for everything that happens around me. God freed me from my guilt.

But there have been times that I really was at fault. When I was first learning about God, and I was beginning to grow in my new-found relationship with Christ, I was eager to learn everything I could about him and His word. I was like a sponge, absorbing all of the information I could get about God and about Christianity. One day, while I was visiting my mom, I came across a book that she had been reading. It was a question-and-answer book about the Bible, and I just had to read it. I asked my mom if I could borrow it. She said she wasn't done with it, but then she agreed to let me take it home for a while, if I promised to bring it back. She died two weeks later, before I had a chance to return it to her.

Now, the whole time I was growing up, my parents never read scripture, went to church, or discussed religion. In fact, one of the worst beatings I ever got was for reading the Genesis account of creation to my brother, from a Bible a friend had given me. My step-dad was furious! So, I should have sensed that it was out of the ordinary for my mom to even own such a book. I can't begin to describe the guilt I felt for taking away what I believed was my mom's last chance to connect with her Savior before she died.

But I had to forgive myself. I knew that God would not have taken her life if she hadn't had sufficient time and information to make a firm decision whether or not to believe and be saved. If she still had questions, I was certain that God would have sent the answers she needed before she died, even though I interfered. God wasn't surprised by my actions; He knows everything. And I am certainly not powerful enough to change God's plans for the salvation of even one of His children. So, again, I found peace, or, perhaps, the peace of God found me.

It is impossible to have peace in our hearts if we are feeling guilty about some misdeed in the past. Guilt certainly has its place, but it is only beneficial if it motivates us to correct a wrong we have done. If it is not possible to correct the problem, such as when the offended party is no longer around to offer forgiveness, it is pointless to allow the guilt to grow or to continue to work on the conscience. When we feel guilty about issues over which we have no control, this tends to inhibit our spiritual growth. Although guilt can be a wonderful tool to prompt us to make changes, it is also easily manipulated by the evil one and overused to our detriment.

We cannot accept God's grace and His gift of forgiveness, if we are unwilling to let go of the past and to forgive ourselves for our own mistakes. We must remember that if God can forgive a sin such as ours, then we certainly can forgive it as well. We must give it to God and allow Him to bury it in the sea with the rest of our sins and not bring it back to mind. So, when the ugly head of guilt rises to condemn us for a forgiven mistake, as it surely will, remember that God has already dealt with it and again give it up to God. Only when we can do this will we be able to move on in our quest for inner peace.

WHAT PEACE IS NOT

So far, we have spent much time discussing how forgiving ourselves and others can bring us closer to having God's peace in our lives. This is an important step, but there is so much more to learn. It would be good, at this time, to take a step back and discover exactly what peace is, and also what it is not.

When I first began my quest for God's peace, I expected that once I found it, I would have a life free from problems, conflict, and trials; a life of complete tranquility and relaxation. Boy was I mistaken! In my study, I have not found even one text in which God promises a stress-free life, at least while we are living here on earth. Instead, I found that we are in the midst of a cosmic conflict between good and evil, and we live on a planet plagued with all sorts of troubles, both physical and spiritual. In 1 Peter 5:8, 9 we read, "Be self-controlled and alert. Your enemy the devil prowls around like a roaring lion looking for someone to devour. Resist him, standing firm in the faith, because you know that your brothers throughout the world are undergoing the same kind of sufferings" (NIV). Clearly, we are all under constant attack from our enemy. No wonder we feel so stressed out at times!

Reading further, we find that anywhere and at any time, we can expect to have trials. Again, Peter tells us, "Dear friends, don't be surprised at the fiery trials you are going through, as if something strange were happening to you. Instead, be very glad—because these trials will make you partners with Christ in his suffering, and afterward you will have the wonderful joy of sharing his glory when it is displayed to all the world" (1 Peter 4:12, 13, NLT). This is a powerful text, packed full of information to help us in our quest to understand peace. It tells us that all of our suffering is not something strange; rather it is common, so common, in fact, that everyone experiences it.

I have found it to be very comforting to know that everyone experiences stress and conflict, and that it isn't just me. There are times when I am so overwhelmed by the pressures of my job, my desires to be a good parent and wife, and my drive to be the best at everything I do, that I begin to question my sanity! I struggle with the many challenges of my day-to-day life, and I sometimes find myself consumed with worry about some of the underlying concerns of our society, such as our current war with Iraq, the possibility of financial peril, and the thought of our kids bringing weapons into our schools. It is difficult, at times, not to get bogged down with anxiety. What a comfort to know that even when the world seems to be so lost, God is aware and has a plan!

This verse also leads us to connect with Christ, who experienced many of the same trials and difficulties that we go through today. He had to suffer beyond what any ordinary man or woman would ever want to have to endure, even to the point of torture and death, for someone else's sin (ours). He is certainly able to understand and sympathize with us, isn't He? Look also at the instruction to "be very glad" for our troubles. That is unquestionably one of the most difficult tasks to accomplish. It is hard to even imagine being glad for any trial that we may have to face. But the rest of the verse gives us reason to try this; we can be glad because we have something better to look forward to, which is the joy of sharing in His glory.

This is further explained by Paul in his letter to the Romans, "…but we also rejoice in our sufferings, because we know that suffering produces perseverance; perseverance, character; and character, hope. And hope does not disappoint us, because God has poured out his love into our hearts by the Holy Spirit, whom he has given us" (Romans 5:3-5, NIV). So, it is through suffering that our character is developed, through the love of God, to help us to be ready for eternal life with Him. Some lessons must simply be learned the hard way, through sweat and tears, in order for us to learn them and become the people God has intended us to be. And He gives us the Holy Spirit to assure our success!

It wasn't long ago that God put me through a series of just such "character-building" experiences. Four months after I started working at a local nursing home, which I was really beginning to love, the company that I worked for decided not to renew the lease on our building. The owner came in and told us all that we had 30 days to find new homes for all of our patients, and we would need to look for new jobs. I was shocked and devastated! I was used to making my own choices about my employment, and I always had a new position before I would leave the current one. It was also a very emotional experience to uproot my patients, some of whom had lived in that facility for many years.

Just a few days later, my husband's father was in a devastating motorcycle accident and was seriously and permanently injured. It was a heartbreaking experience for my entire family. If that wasn't enough, my grandmother, the only person from my childhood that I knew really loved me, passed away just a few months later. This pushed me to my breaking point. To top it off, I then developed a serious medical condition myself and needed surgery.

I remember telling God that I just couldn't take any more. I pleaded with Him to make it stop. I reminded Him of His promises in the scriptures not to tempt me beyond what I was able to bear and to provide a way out for me if I needed it. Well, I needed it!

As I began to open up and be honest with God, I was able to let Him share in my burdens. It took a long time to let it all go and allow Him to handle it. As I realized that it was not me that was in control of my life, but God who had the master plan, I was able to experience peace within my soul. I began to see the lessons that He had for me, and I began to grow spiritually. I started to learn to trust Him more and not to rely on my own strength and power to get me through. God was there for me once again.

James tells us: "My brethren, count it all joy when you fall into various trials, knowing that the testing of your faith produces patience. But let patience have its perfect work, that you may be perfect and complete, lacking nothing" (James 1:2-4, NKJV). We need to change our perspective and stop seeing our troubles as punishment from God or God not understanding our needs. Rather, we need to see that our troubles are a blessing; God counts us as so valuable that He will work as long and as hard as it takes to perfect our character so that we can be with Him throughout eternity. When I looked for the lessons in my trials, I could learn from them.

This discipline, which means to make a disciple, or to teach, is much different from punishment. Sometimes, it may take several attempts, even years of struggle, before we get it right. Perseverance and the grace of God will prevail, and we will make it through our troubles and be better off for overcoming them. Each test that we pass, each temptation that we defeat, each lesson we learn, brings us one step closer to what Christ has in store for us.

Even Christ had to experience this kind of character building, although I believe it was for our benefit, rather than His, that he endured it. After all, He was our ultimate example, being tested just as we are and showing us how to overcome all things. Hebrews 5:8 says, "So even though Jesus was God's Son, he learned obedience from the things he suffered" (NLT). We should not be surprised, then, when God allows us to learn things the hard way.

As another example, in Isaiah 38, we read the story of King Hezekiah, who faced a serious trial. He was sick and dying, and as he felt the gravity of the situation, he begged the Lord to spare his life. The Lord heard his prayer, felt his tears and his pain, and had compassion on the king. He promised to let Hezekiah live another 15 years, and He even gave him a sign that He would heal him, by making the sun go backward. When the king recovered, he praised God, and said, "...surely it was for my benefit that I suffered such anguish. In your love you kept me from the pit of destruction; you have put all my sins behind your back" (Isaiah 38:17, NIV). Even the king recognized that there was a reason for his suffering. Of course, we always see more clearly when we come through our troubles to the other side and can look back and see how different things may have been had we taken a different path.

Paul also tells us, in 2 Corinthians 1:8, 9 (NLT) that he was severely tested:

"I think you ought to know, dear brothers and sisters, about the trouble we went through in the province of Asia. We were crushed and completely overwhelmed, and we thought we would never live through it. In fact, we expected to die. But as a result, we learned not to rely on ourselves, but on God who can raise the dead." He goes on to explain the blessings he and his companions received and how he learned that he can always count on God.

I think the ultimate biblical example of a trail was given to Abraham. He had a very special relationship with God. He was even called "God's friend" (James 2:23). God had promised to make him a father of many nations and to bless his family for generations. It was through Abraham's descendants that the promised Messiah was to come. Abraham knew this and was pleased. He trusted God and was faithful. Then something strange happened. "Take your son, your only son, Isaac, whom you love, and go to the region of Moriah. Sacrifice him there as a burnt offering on one of the mountains I will tell you about" (Genesis 22:2, NIV).

Talk about a test! If I heard God tell me to take one of my children and offer him or her as a sacrifice, I would think I had lost my mind and I would go directly to a psychiatrist! Abraham didn't even question it. He didn't argue with God, though he could have; he had done that before.

Remember the story of Sodom and Gomorrah? God told Abraham that He was going to destroy Sodom, and Abraham questioned Him, "Would you also destroy the righteous with the wicked? Suppose there were fifty righteous within the city; would You also destroy the place and not spare it for the fifty righteous that were in it?" (Genesis 18: 23, 24, NKJV). He began to bargain with God. God agreed not to destroy the city if there were 50 righteous. Then he talked him down to 45, then 40, 30, 20, and finally ten. If there were even ten righteous people in Sodom, surely God would spare the city. Abraham, no doubt, was thinking about his nephew, Lot, and his family, who were living in Sodom at the time. Wouldn't Lot and his family have had enough influence on their neighbors and friends that God would find at least ten righteous people in Sodom? But, you know the outcome. The city was destroyed, and only Lot and his two daughters survived the ordeal.

Abraham was not afraid to confront God about his request. He could have argued, "God, you promised me a blessing through my son. I have waited a lifetime for him, and now you want to take him from me? I don't understand. You can't possibly want me to do this. Besides, you detest human sacrifices. This doesn't make any sense..." But Abraham didn't argue. He didn't question God. He just took Isaac, some wood for the offering, and his knife. He went up to the mountain that God had shown him. Even when Isaac asked his father where the lamb was, Abraham stayed true to his calling. His faith was unwavering. He tied Isaac up, put him on the altar, arranged the wood, lifted the knife, and was ready to give everything dear to him, when God stopped him and provided a ram in Isaac's place. Abraham had passed the test.

If God's faithful servant, his friend, could be tested in such a way, how can we think that we should have it any easier? God knows our hearts, and he knows exactly what it will take to make us fit for heaven. What he will ask from me is different from what he will ask from you, but, make no mistake, he will be asking each of us to give whatever it takes to help us grow spiritually, so that his grace can be revealed in our lives. Each trial we encounter, each temptation that we overcome, not only improves our own character, but displays God's grace to the universe.

Another lesson we can learn from our temptations can be found in the example of King David. David was an impulsive and moody guy. Read the psalms, and you will understand what I mean. He was also counted among the righteous listed in Hebrews 11:32. He lived anything but a perfect, serene life. He made some really big mistakes, but God still counted him as faithful. David knew about temptation. In 2 Samuel, chapter 11, we read the story of David and Bathsheba: There was David, taking an afternoon stroll on his roof. He was admiring his city, and suddenly a beautiful woman bathing on her roof caught his eye. What a sight! Now, remember that David was king. He had plenty of women around: wives, concubines, servants. He didn't need another woman to satisfy him. But she was so beautiful! He had to meet her. He asked around, and found out who she was and sent for her. He was well aware of her marital status, and he should have known better than to even start something with her, but he got caught up in his lustful desires. He seduced her into an adulterous relationship. She got pregnant! So, what was the man to do? Would he confess his sin to her husband and beg for forgiveness? Did he offer to care for her and make things right? No, not David! He sets up an elaborate scheme to cover the whole thing up. The problem was that Uriah, her husband, didn't fall for it, and the plan backfired. So David, in his own wisdom, did the next best thing and had Uriah killed. Problem solved, right? Not exactly.

I am so glad that this story is in the Bible. God could have easily left this story out. He could have led us to believe that David was perfect in every way, and that we would have to be perfect to be counted righteous. But he doesn't. He gives us this story so that we can know that as sinful and as easily led astray by temptation that we tend to be, He is still with us, and He still loves us. If we read further, we find that David's mistake didn't just go away. He suffered greatly, and so did his entire family, because of his indiscretion. God didn't hold back the consequences of David's mistake. Life was not easy for David. The struggles continued throughout his life. So, this is the perfect example for us.

We make mistakes. We have to live with the consequences of the mistakes we make. Sometimes we suffer the consequences of others' mistakes. That's the way it is on planet earth. But our trials, temptations, and difficulties are not a result of God's anger or abandonment. He does not stop loving us or caring about us, or even protecting and guiding us, because of our sins. He has already paid the penalty for our sins. His forgiveness is available to us before we even ask. He remains by our side, to help us when we need him. He will go to any length to show his love for this fallen race and for each of us, individually. So, when you feel like you have really messed up, and that you are not good enough, remember the "faithful" and the problems they faced. God did not abandon them in their time of need, but gave them the ability to press on in the face of great obstacles. And he counted their faith as righteousness. He is willing to do the same for us.

So, the next time you are tested, tempted, tried, disciplined, or troubled, do not be discouraged; remember that God is with you and that "…all things work together for good to those who love God…" (Romans 8:28, NKJV). Also remember that we can and will experience conflict throughout our lives. This is normal. Even so, we can experience God's peace in the midst of our troubles, if we do not lose sight of God's immense love for us, and we continue to trust in His ability to guide and protect us.

TRUST

How can I trust you and know that you will care,
If I open up my heart to you, my dreams and fears to share?
Are you really with me? I cannot see your face.
I hear stories of your mercy; I long to know your grace.
Do you really understand my longings and my pain,
The questions and the thoughts that are racing through my brain?
I want to know and trust you, my Savior and my friend,
But my fears stand in-between us. Your love, will it transcend?
Can I give up my selfishness, put away my pride,
With full understanding that you're always by my side?
You say that you are with me. You ask me to trust and obey.
My inner thoughts, however, tell me to turn away.
I give you my sorrows, my troubles, and my pain
Only to reach out and take them back again.
I challenge you at every turn. I don't want to submit.
But you are kind and patient. You will not let me quit!
You send me needed trials, which help me more to grow.
You push me to my limits, so your love I can fully know.
As I practice letting go, and trusting you with each step,
I learn that you are faithful, with every promise kept.
You are worthy of my trust, unlike people I know here.
You want only what is best for me, and I have nothing to fear.
How can I know? You gave everything you had.
Your son's own blood was spilled for me, so I could call you "Dad."

WHAT IS PEACE ?

So, if peace is not about having a trouble-free life, then what, exactly, is it? First of all, it is a gift from Christ, "Peace I leave with you, My peace I give to you; not as the world gives do I give to you. Let not your heart be troubled, neither let it be afraid" (John 14:27, NKJV). Obviously, peace is something special that Christ wants us to have, and when we have it, we will not be afraid. His gift, however, is different from the gifts of this world. "…you will experience God's peace, which is far more wonderful than the human mind can understand. His peace will guard your hearts and minds as you live in Christ Jesus" (Philippians 4:7, NLT). Wow! It is more wonderful than our minds can understand! This sounds like something worth pursuing, doesn't it?

Again, "I have told you these things, so that in me you may have peace. In this world you will have trouble. But take heart! I have overcome the world" (John 16:33, NIV). Peace is not the absence of trouble. It is a way of *coping with trouble.* It is through our faith in Christ that we gain the power to overcome and thereby obtain the gift of peace. For me, having peace is like knowing, at the end of a particularly stressful day, as the kids are fighting, things aren't going well at work, and I am feeling tired and grumpy, that somehow it is still okay. It is knowing that God is ultimately in control, and all the annoyances that are stressing me out are really insignificant. It is when God tells me, "You are my child. I care about you. Lean on Me, and I will get you through this." This is a gift, indeed.

Peace is associated with other gifts throughout the scriptures as well. Paul writes in his letter to the Romans: "So I pray that God, who gives you hope, will keep you happy and full of peace as you believe in him. May you overflow with hope through the power of the Holy Spirit" (Romans 15:13, NLT). Here, peace is mentioned along with hope, as something that will keep us happy. Hope is an important part of having peace. We have hope that things will be better tomorrow. We have hope that God will bless us when we trust Him. We have hope in eternal life through Christ and with Christ in heaven. It is hope that motivates us to keep pushing on when things get tough. Hope stirs a fire within our hearts and encourages us. This is part of having peace.

Jeremiah 33:6 states, "...I will heal my people and will let them enjoy abundant peace and security" (NIV). In this text, peace is paired with security. Security is one of our most basic needs. We need to know we are safe. I have always had difficulty sleeping. I think it stems from my childhood, when I was not safe in my bed at night. Sometimes my step father would sneak into my room to "cuddle" and then some. Even after I left home and married, I was not safe. I lived in bad neighborhoods, with drug dealers and gunshots to worry me at night. My first husband would also cause me to feel unsafe at night. He would do strange things, like take the furniture apart, looking for "bugs" (the listening kind, not the insect kind). Sometimes, he would wander around outside doing who-knows-what in the middle of the night. Then there were the times that he would stand in the doorway of our bedroom and watch me. Have you ever tried to sleep with someone staring at you? I don't know how, but it is as if I could feel it, and I certainly couldn't sleep.

In any case, when I remarried and moved into a beautiful new home in the country, I adopted two precious puppies. They grew into big, cuddly dogs, but they are also very protective. I know that there is no way someone can sneak up on us to rob us or harm us in any way without our knowing it well ahead of time. They are the best alarm system I could have bought. Now I can sleep. God uses a variety of methods to help give us a sense of security in our lives. For me it is my dogs. Security is part of having peace.

In Isaiah we find: "And the work of righteousness shall be peace; and the effect of righteousness quietness and assurance forever" (Isaiah 32:17, KJV). Righteousness is right-doing. It is obeying God. We have peace by obeying God, knowing that He is pleased when we make right choices. We feel good when we know we are doing the right thing. Quietness and assurance are the result. We don't have the inner turmoil and guilty feelings that we should have made a better choice. We are sure of ourselves and feel right with God. This, too, is peace.

So, we have peace, righteousness, hope, happiness, belief, security, quietness, and assurance all working together in those who follow Christ. But this still doesn't tell us exactly what peace is or how to get it. But we are not left in the dark, without direction. We are shown the way to understanding and gaining God's peace in many places throughout the Bible.

One thing we need to do to receive this gift is to fix our minds on God. "You will keep him in perfect peace, whose mind is stayed on You, because he trusts in You" (Isaiah 26:3, NKJV). Thinking about God and trusting Him are important. We must know in our heart of hearts that God is who He says He is and that He will do what He says He will do. This is trust. We also need to follow God's instructions: "My son, forget not my law; but let thine heart keep my commandments; for length of days, and long life, and peace, shall they add to thee" (Proverbs 3:1, 2, KJV). Again, "If only you had paid attention to my commands, your peace would have been like a river, your righteousness like the waves of the sea" (Isaiah 48:18, NIV). The opposite is also true: "'There is no peace,' says the Lord, "for the wicked" (vs. 22). Referring to wisdom, Solomon tells us, "Her ways are ways of pleasantness, and all her paths are peace"

(Proverbs 3:17, NKJV). So, if we seek God, follow his commandments, and exercise wisdom, we will begin to experience God's peace.

We must also surrender our hearts to Christ, "The mind of the sinful man is death, but the mind controlled by the Spirit is life and peace" (Romans 8:6, NIV). So often, our choices are tough to make. We know we ought to do one thing, but we really want to do something else. We need to rely on the Holy Spirit during these difficult times, to help us see past immediate gratification to the end result of our choices. When we choose to do what is right, we have satisfaction and peace. Often we cannot make these choices in our own strength, so it is imperative that we seek God's counsel often and with our hearts open to His guidance.

Furthermore, in Acts 10:36 we read: "I am sure you have heard about the Good News for the people of Israel—that there is peace with God through Jesus Christ, who is Lord of all" (NLT). Again, Colossians 3:15 says, "And let the peace that comes from Christ rule in your hearts. For as members of one body you are all called to live in peace..." (NLT). So, peace is something that comes from Christ, something that affects our minds, something that can rule and control our hearts and be projected in our lives. It appears that peace is so much more than the absence of conflict. It is a deeply felt condition of the heart in which Christ rules and our lives are somehow transformed. And, it is something from God that we have access to simply by believing in God and developing trust in Him.

Christ not only gives us peace, but the Bible tells us that he *is* peace. Micah 5:5 states: "And he will be the source of our peace..." (NLT). Again, "May God himself, the God of peace..." (1 Thessalonians 5:23, NIV), and Ephesians 2:14: "For he himself is our peace..."(NIV). Furthermore, it is through the cross that Christ offers us peace. He was our perfect sacrifice, he made the way for us to have eternal life and be freed from our sins. This very thought should bring to us the peace of knowing that we are forever released from the bondage of sin, so that we may have assurance during our toughest trials. 1Peter 1:18,19 says, "For you know that it was not with perishable things such as silver or gold that you were redeemed from the empty way of life handed down to you from your forefathers, but with the precious blood of Christ, a lamb without blemish or defect," (NIV). He was our redeemer, our way out of our sins and into salvation. Isaiah 53:5 says, "But he was wounded and crushed for our sins. He was beaten that we might have peace. He was whipped, and we were healed!" (NLT). He took our sins and left us peace in their place! Again, we read in Romans 5:1, "Therefore, having been justified by faith, we have peace with God through our Lord Jesus Christ" (NKJV). The knowledge and understanding of our salvation brings us peace with God. Once more, "…and by him God reconciled everything to himself. He made peace with everything in heaven and on earth by means of his blood on the cross" (Colossians 1:20, NLT). This peace of salvation reaches even beyond us and into all creation! What an amazing gift!

To illustrate the kind of peace that comes from understanding salvation, look at the story of Daniel's three friends in Daniel, chapter 3. The King had made for himself a golden statue that was set up on the open plain for everyone in the land to see. He made a law that when the music played, all the people in the land were to bow themselves in worship to the statue. The king's servants reported back to the king that there were 3 Jewish men who refused to worship the king's gods or his statue, which made the king furious. He sent for the men and asked them if the charges were true. He gave them the chance to follow his law, but if they refused, they were to be thrown into a furnace and burned to death. Their reply to the king is a perfect example of the peace that comes from trusting God and accepting his gift of salvation:

"…O Nebuchadnezzar, we do not need to defend ourselves before you in this matter. If we are thrown into the blazing furnace, the God we serve *is able to save us from it, and he will rescue us from your hand, O king. But even if he does not, we want you to know, O king, that we will not serve your gods or worship the image of gold you have set up"* (vv. 16-18, NIV).

They did not know if they would be saved from death in the furnace. They only knew that God could save them, if that was His choice. They also knew that it didn't matter in the larger scheme of things, as they were assured of an eternal life after this one, so they were not afraid of death. Now that is peace! This was not an absence of conflict. I am sure the men wondered what would happen. But they were secure in their faith that God would not let them down, no matter how things ended up. If you don't know the end result, please read the rest of the chapter. God didn't let them down.

God wants nothing more than for us to trust Him enough that we will accept the gift of peace that he offers us, and to share it with others. He wants us to crave it, and He wants to give it to us. Psalm 34:14 tells us to "Depart from evil and do good; seek peace and pursue it" (NKJV). Also, 2 Timothy 2:22 says, "Run from anything that stimulates youthful lust. Follow anything that makes you want to do right. Pursue faith and love and peace, and enjoy the companionship of those who call on the Lord with pure hearts" (NLT). This is a gift worth seeking.

God calls us to share this gift with others. In the Sermon on the Mount, Christ tells the people: "Blessed are the peacemakers: for they shall be called the children of God" (Matthew 5:9, KJV). Proverbs 12:20 says, "There is deceit in the hearts of those who plot evil, but joy for those who promote peace" (NIV), and James says,

"But the wisdom that comes from heaven is first of all pure. It is also peace loving, gentle at all times, and willing to yield to others. It is full

of mercy and good deeds. It shows no partiality and is always sincere. And those who are peacemakers will plant seeds of peace and reap a harvest of goodness" (James 3: 17, 18, NLT).

When we understand, accept, and share God's peace, we will spread goodness. What a promise!

This is what Jesus has to offer. He shared it with His disciples, and He shares it with us. Luke 24:36 shows us His wish: "Now as they said these things, Jesus Himself stood in the midst of them, and said to them, "Peace to you" (NKJV). All we have to do is accept the gift. He is waiting. Are you ready?

IN CONTROL

Sometimes I feel like I'm on top of my game.
I have all the answers; I'm feeling no shame.
Sometimes, though, it's as if the entire world
Is crashing down around me, as it comes unfurled.

I try to be strong, to handle it all on my own.
I don't need anyone's help, not if my weaknesses will be known.
But, truth be told, I really can't do it all by myself.
I need to reach out and ask others for help.

Whenever someone else needs assistance from me,
I'm there in a flash, to help selflessly.
But accepting the same from someone else
Requires admitting I can't do it all myself.

So, "letting go" and "letting God" are the most difficult tasks.
Much harder than anything else that He asks.
So instead, I take on the world and its troubles
Without letting Him help me, until the stress doubles.

Then I cry out, "Lord, please give me a hand!"
So that when I crash, there's a soft place to land.
Perhaps someday I will stop trying to maintain control
And just accept the peace He offers and rejoice, Oh my soul.

A SABBATH REST

So, now that we have learned a little about God's gift of peace, let's begin to focus more on how we can experience it. God has given us a wonderful gift that helps in our quest for peace. It is His gift of time. The Bible calls this gift the Sabbath.

If you recall the Genesis account of creation, God created the earth and everything in it in six days. At the completion of each day, God critiqued his work and declared that "it is good" (Genesis 1). When he crowned his work of creation with the introduction of mankind into the world, He "saw that it was excellent in every way" (Genesis 1:31, NLT). Then, on the seventh day, the Bible tells us, God rested.

Now, I am certain that God was not resting because He was tired and needed a break. He was taking time to stop working and to reflect on and appreciate his creation. He wanted to enjoy the result of his labors, just as an artist steps back to admire his work when he is finished creating it. God blessed this day and made it holy. This was to be a special time to reflect, to enjoy, and to rest from work. God set aside this time the very day after mankind was created, with our needs already on his mind. His blessing was to be extended to us and repeated week after week throughout eternity, as a time of rest for our weary hearts, a time to meet with our creator, and a time to stop our frantic busyness and to reflect on all that is good.

Have you ever noticed that the commandment that God gave us regarding this rest starts with the word "remember" (Exodus 20:8)? Do you think that God knew all along that we would get so busy trying to get the most out of our work, our finances, our relationships, and our leisure time, that we would forget to stop once in a while and rest and reflect on the things He has done for us? Maybe He understood about deadlines, overtime, chores, soccer practice, piano lessons, Karate classes, parent-teacher conferences, doctor appointments, automobile repair, business trips, band recitals, home improvement projects and the like. Maybe He knew it was our nature to squeeze just one more thing into our busy schedules, until we were only sleeping five hours a night. Do we schedule time for God, too? Perhaps we spare a few minutes in the morning before we rush out the door, late for work. Maybe we say a quick prayer in bed at night as we begin to doze off. Don't forget grace at dinner, and the two hours at church each week, if we don't have more pressing obligations. That counts, doesn't it?

But is this God's plan for our relationship with him? Do you think this is what He really wants? I dare say not. He has set aside a full 24 hours each week just to spend with us. Sure, we can come to Him at any time, and He will be there. He is with us at all times. But, He has set aside a special, holy time, to help us meet with Him in a special way. Jesus said, "The Sabbath was made to benefit people, and not people to benefit the Sabbath" (Mark 2:27, NLT).

Yes, God understands our need for a time of rest and quiet reflection. That is why Christ bids us to "Come unto me, all ye that labour and are heavy laden, and I will give you rest" (Matthew 11:28, KJV). He wants only what is best for us. Imagine taking a vacation every single week! God gives us a whole day to stop fretting about the troubles of the week and worrying about how to meet all of the demands on our time and resources, and instead to concentrate on the amazing grace of our heavenly father.

Every week, I look forward to the Sabbath. I work so hard at my job and in my home, trying to keep everything running smoothly and assuring that everyone's needs are met. I push myself to be the best I can be at everything I do. Sometimes, it is absolutely overwhelming. But because of my promise to God to keep His Sabbath day holy, I can look forward to an entire day each and every week, in which I can relax and experience God's presence without all of the distractions and pressures of the rest of the week. I can be free to be myself. I can let go of all of the concerns of my job, the countless chores that never seem to get done, and the multitude of insignificant things that take up my time.

I can use this time to go on hikes and reconnect with the sights, smells, and sounds of nature, that call me back to a less hectic time, and remind me of the awesome, creative power of God. I can use the time to connect with my family, especially my teenagers, who need to know that I'm there for them, even if they are operating in "silent mode". I can spend time in fellowship, getting to know the rest of my church family. This is a time to concentrate more on relationships and less on tasks. We all need time together, interacting with, understanding, and encouraging one another.

Somehow, in all of our busyness, our relationships tend to suffer. We become hermits or slaves to our schedules. We get out of touch with even our closest friends and wonder, "Where has all the time gone?" When we allow ourselves to set aside time each week to practice love for one another, by spending time together, it refreshes our souls. We are desperate for this connection with God and with each other, and the Sabbath provides us an excellent opportunity to grow in our relationships.

Often, when someone mentions the Sabbath, we tend to think of it as a burden, in which God restricts us from doing the things we want to do. Back in Jesus' day, the religious leaders had so many rules and regulations about what could and could not be done that it truly became such a burden. There were rules about how far a person could walk, restrictions on building a fire, cooking, and picking food to eat, and regulations about every minute detail of daily living. These rules defined the tasks that constituted work and those which were to be allowed; they were not part of the scriptural law, which was given to man by God, but were simply regulations that the priests had made up in their own interpretation of God's law. Jesus confronted the rulers on several occasions about the foolishness of their over regulation of his divine law. He prepared and ate grain on the Sabbath, He healed on the Sabbath, and He even told them that He was Lord of the Sabbath.

Picture this: Jesus and His disciples were walking along through the fields of grain, when they reached out and picked a few kernels. They rolled them between their hands, blew away the hulls, and began to eat. This was not a great feast, and it took little effort to prepare. It was raw, dry, dusty grain; one would think they must have been pretty hungry before they would want to eat that. The Pharisees were quick to point out to Jesus that His disciples were breaking the law by "working" on the Sabbath. Jesus retorted that there were stories in the scriptures, the ones they were supposed to revere so much, that told of David and his companions eating bread from the tabernacle, which was set aside for the priests. He also pointed out that the priests in the temple were innocent when they worked on the Sabbath. Then He told them that there was "One" present that was greater than the temple, and He quoted scripture to them stating that mercy is better than sacrifice, and finally that He, himself, was Lord of the Sabbath!

Continuing on from the field, Jesus and the disciples proceeded into the temple. He found a man there with a deformed hand. The Pharisees saw Him notice the man, and they asked Jesus if healing on the Sabbath was lawful. They were, of course, trying to trick Him into saying something they could use against Him. He answered them that if they had a sheep which fell into a well on the

Sabbath, that they would surely rescue it. He told them that people are more valuable than sheep, so it would be legal to do good deeds on the Sabbath. Then he healed the man's hand right in front of them. (Matthew 12: 1-14). God is not concerned with man's interpretations of His law. The Sabbath means much more for us than a list of restrictions and regulations that would be impossible for us to follow. Christ demonstrated the love and compassion that God has for us in healing on the Sabbath day.

Isaiah 58: 13, 14 tells us, *"Keep the Sabbath day holy. Don't pursue your own interests on that day, but enjoy the Sabbath and speak of it with delight as the Lord's holy day. Honor the Lord in everything you do, and don't follow your own desires or talk idly. If you do this, the Lord will be your delight. I will give you great honor and give you your full share of the inheritance I promised to Jacob, your ancestor. I, the Lord, have spoken!"* (NLT).

So, when God set aside the Sabbath day for us, he meant it for our pleasure. He knew what a blessing it would be for us to spend time with Him, getting to know Him better. He asks us not to do our ordinary, everyday work, so that we will be free to enjoy His presence. If we are willing to spend this time with Him each week, He will help us to free up this time, so that we can concentrate on our relationship with Him. He also gave us an amazing example of what He is willing to do for us and how important this time is to Him. We pick up the story in Exodus Ch 16:

The Israelites were living in the desert at this time. They were hungry and they were grumbling to Moses that they were better off in Egypt, where at least they had food to eat. The Lord heard their complaints and promised to send them bread. He told the people to go out in the morning and gather enough manna, which was a thin flake of bread that looked like frost and tasted like honey, to last them through that day only. On the sixth day of the week, they were to gather twice as much as they would need, and they were not to gather any on the Sabbath. He also promised them meat in the evening.

Sure enough, that evening, the camp was filled with quail for them to eat, and in the morning, after the dew lifted, there was manna everywhere on the ground, ready to be gathered for that day's food. The Israelites gathered the manna, as they were told. Whatever was not gathered melted away as the day warmed up. Some of them took more than they needed, however, and they kept it until the next morning. When they awoke, the leftover manna stunk and was full of maggots. When the sixth day came, the people gathered twice as much manna as they normally did, and it kept without rotting over the course of the Sabbath, and no manna fell on the Sabbath. Some of the people did not keep extra manna on the sixth day, as instructed, but went out on the Sabbath to gather some and found that none had fallen. This cycle went on for forty years, as an example of how the Lord will provide for His people.

Now, you may be thinking that this whole Sabbath concept was a great thing back in its day, but what about today? Does God really expect us to keep this appointment with Him every week, even at this point in history? I believe He does. He has always wanted to be first in our lives, and this is not an outdated concept. He wants us to continue to spend time with Him now, by keeping His Sabbath holy. He even wants this institution to continue in the future, beyond this earth and beyond the time of the Lord's return.

Isaiah 66:22-23 tells us, *"For as the new heavens and the new earth which I will make shall remain before me,' says the Lord, 'so shall your descendants and your name remain. And it shall come to pass that from one New Moon to another, and from one Sabbath to another, all flesh shall come to worship before Me,' says the Lord"* (NKJV).

So, what have you got to lose? Try spending time with God, contemplating His grace, learning of His peace. Keep your appointment with Him. He is waiting for you.

CONTENTMENT

What, exactly, is it that is keeping you from grabbing hold of the peace that God offers you? I would venture that it is fear. Perhaps fear is too strong of a word for you. What about anxiety or worry? Could it be that you worry about making the right decisions, missing opportunities that God puts before you, or choosing the wrong course when the choice needs to be made? If so, I can certainly relate. I often feel like a juggler with dozens of balls all up in the air. I worry that I will drop one, and then all the others will come crashing down around me. If that were to happen, oh my! Then everyone would know my secret: I am human! I certainly wouldn't want that!

When an important decision needs to be made, have you ever found yourself asking, "God, if this is your will, can you give me a sign?" Of course, I wish for my sign to be a billboard along the highway, something unmistakable, something clearly laid out in front of me, so that I could not possibly miss it. More often than not, however, it is just a still, small voice in my head, nudging me in a certain direction. A voice clear enough to be noticed, yet subtle enough that I can, and usually do, argue with it and try to talk my way out of following its promptings.

Does worry interfere with your attempts to have God's peace? We can be thankful that God does not leave us to worry about all of our decisions on our own. The only decision we have to make is to choose to follow Him. He will provide us with everything else. Have you ever thought that maybe there is not a right or wrong choice to be made at every crossroads? Perhaps God is more concerned with the process or the journey that we take than with the minute details of our decisions. After all, our salvation does not necessarily depend on which job we take, what school we go to, or even with whom we associate. God may have a specific plan for us in any of these areas, or, His plan may work out the same, regardless of which way we decide to go. For each of us, His plan will be different, but God is always the same. He wants us to have a relationship with Him and to trust Him in all things. He does not watch over us just to sit in judgment, waiting for us to make a mistake. So, why all the worry?

Matthew 6:25-34 tells us that God does not intend for us to worry about the details of our lives. "Can all your worries add a single moment to your life? Of course not" (v.27, NLT) He promises to provide for all of our needs, "Your heavenly Father already knows all your needs, and he will give you all you need from day to day if you live for him and make the Kingdom of God your primary concern" (v. 33, NLT).

The real key to contentment is being satisfied with what God gives us day to day. So much of our time is spent "chasing after the wind" (Ecclesiastes 2:11), that we lose the perspective of focusing on the blessings of the present. How much more will it take to satisfy us? Do we need more money? Will a bigger house or a fancier car or the hottest fashions finally get us where we want to be? Doubtful. God has planted in us a desire for more important things. Ecclesiastes 5:10 states, "He who loves silver will not be satisfied with silver; nor he who loves abundance, with increase..."(NKJV). Instead, Jeremiah 31:14 tells us, "...my people will be satisfied with my goodness..."(NKJV). We should be always diligently seeking God above all things. Psalms 84:10, 11 states, "A single day in your courts is better than a thousand anywhere else! I would rather be a gatekeeper in the house of my God than live the good life in the homes of the wicked. For the Lord God is our light and protector. He gives us grace and glory. No good thing will the Lord withhold from those who do what is right" (NLT). Isn't it time we stop searching for the treasures of this world and concentrate fully on the real treasure, which is Christ? "But store up for yourselves treasures in heaven, where moth and rust do not destroy, and where thieves do not break in and steal. For where your treasure is, there your heart will be also" (Matthew 6:21, 22 NIV).

Paul reflects a real attitude of peace and acceptance of his place in life, when he tells us, "Not that I was ever in need, for I have learned how to get along happily whether I have much or little. I know how to live on almost nothing or with everything. I have learned the secret of living in every situation, whether it is with a full stomach or empty, with plenty or little. For I can do everything with the help of Christ who gives me the strength I need" (Philippians 4:11-13, NLT). This is exactly the attitude that real Christians should have. If we really trust God to provide for all of our needs, we will not worry about all the insignificant details in our lives that tend to distract us from having true peace. Notice that Paul gets along "happily" in any case. He doesn't grumble and tell everyone how miserable he is. He doesn't ask the "why me?" question. He doesn't feel sorry for himself. He just accepts the situation that God puts him in and is happy about it! Imagine the relief we could feel if we could just accept things when they don't go as we would have them go and could look on the bright side. We could really be at peace. And image what the people around us would think. You know, true joy is contagious!

Recently, I was feeling really overwhelmed and overstressed. My job was difficult, my marriage was rocky, and I was afraid. It was as if everything was crashing down around me. I asked God to change my life. Maybe I needed a new job. Maybe I should move to a sunnier, warmer place. I thought constantly about running away and starting a new life somewhere else. Of course, I didn't know what I would do once I got there, so I waited for God to tell me what to do. God used that still, small voice to remind me that I needed to be patient and things would work out. So, I agreed, begrudgingly, to wait and see what would happen. A month went by, and nothing changed. Finally, I asked God something I had never asked Him before: if He was not going to give me what I wanted, then would He make me want what I already had? What a life-changing request! God answered that prayer and helped me to see all of the blessings He had given me. He helped me to really enjoy my job and my family. He helped me to be more patient, loving, and understanding, where before I was bitter and angry. I became more thankful to God and aware of His presence in every area of my life.

Solomon understood this awareness. In Ecclesiastes 6:9, he advises: "Enjoy what you have rather than desiring what you don't have. Just dreaming about nice things is meaningless; it is like chasing the wind" (NLT). Imagine yourself being content with exactly what you have, right now, instead of putting off your happiness until you have achieved some distant goal or have obtained enough material gain to satisfy you. "Do not boast about tomorrow, for you do not know what a day may bring forth" (Proverbs 27:1, NIV). If we put off our happiness until some future date or event, can we really be assured of reaching that point? Why waste what we have right now, waiting for something to change in the future? We have no assurance that we will live past the next traffic light or see tomorrow. Carpe Diem! (Seize the day!)

Learning to live for the moment is a lofty goal, but one well worth our efforts. Paul tells us in 1 Timothy 6:6-10:

> *"Now godliness with contentment is great gain. For we brought nothing into this world, and it is certain we can carry nothing out. And having food and clothing, with these we shall be content. But those who desire to be rich fall into temptation and a snare, and into many foolish and harmful lusts which drown men in destruction and perdition. For the*

love of money is a root of all kinds of evil, for which some have strayed from the faith in their greediness, and pierced themselves through with many sorrows" (NKJV).

Again, we are encouraged to be happy with what we have, because the relentless drive for more and more often leads us down paths that take us away from God and his plans for our lives.

So, what are we to do if things aren't going exactly well in our lives? How can we be happy and content with our situations, in that case?

"But he said to me, 'My grace is sufficient for you, for my power is made perfect in weakness.' Therefore I will boast all the more gladly about my weaknesses, so that Christ's power may rest on me. That is why, for Christ's sake, I delight in weaknesses, in insults, in hardships, in persecutions, in difficulties. For when I am weak, then I am strong" (2 Corinthians 12:9, 10, NIV).

We cannot always control the situations that we find ourselves in, but we can always control our own attitudes toward our circumstances. We can choose to be negative and whine and complain, or we can choose to make the best of it and thank God for his power to work things out for us in His time.

This brings us back again to trust. We need to fully trust God to take control and help us to make sense of it all. He promises to be with us in everything. He promises to meet our needs. We need to trust him. After all, He is the one in control. He has plans for each of us, and He will continue to guide us along the path that he lays out ahead of us. Philippians 1:6 tells us, "being confident of this, that he who began a good work in you will carry it on to completion until the day of Christ Jesus" (NIV). "Furthermore, because of Christ, we have received an inheritance from God, for he chose us from the beginning, and all things happen just as he decided long ago" (Ephesians 1:11, NLT).

God really has a plan, and it includes every one of us that will listen to His call and follow him. All we have to do is listen to Him and learn to trust Him. Since He has the plan, and since He has the power, what have we got to lose by trusting the details to Him?

I know that takes patience. We need to remind ourselves constantly that things will work out at the proper time. "And we know that in all things God works for the good of those who love him, who have been called according to his purpose" (Romans 8:28, NIV). Ecclesiastes 3:1 states, "There is a time for everything, and a season for every activity under heaven..." (NIV). God's timing, not ours, is the one we must respect. "So, don't get tired of doing what is good. Don't get discouraged and give up, for we will reap a harvest of blessing at the appropriate time" (Galatians 6:9, NLT).

I think this is the hardest part for most of us. We want things to work out now, according to our own time table. We don't want to be patient. We are used to instant gratification, and we don't like having to wait for anything. In our TV generation, most problems are solved in 30-60 minutes. The more complex ones take 120 minutes. Who has time to wait months, or even years, for God to fix our blunders? But God's timetable is much different. He invented patience. "But, beloved, be not ignorant of this one thing, that one day is with the Lord as a thousand years, and a thousand years as one day" (2 Peter 3:8, KJV). If we trust God and allow His plan to work out in its own time, we will truly find peace, but when we become impatient and look for quick fixes to our problems, we begin to struggle.

This reminds me of Lot's wife. You can find the story in Genesis chapter 19. Lot was living in Sodom, a very wicked city. Two angels met Lot at the city gate. Lot greeted them and invited them home for dinner. As they were finishing up and preparing for bed, the men from the city surrounded his house and began rioting, insisting that the two men (angels) be sent out to them, for sexual purposes. Lot stepped outside and intervened in the men's behalf, even going as far as to offer his virgin daughters in order to protect the angels from harm. The men outside were furious and would have killed Lot, but the angels reached out and grabbed him, pulling him back inside and locking the door, then struck the mob with blindness. The angels then asked Lot to prepare his family to leave, for they had been sent to destroy this wicked city.

Lot hurried to tell his potential sons-in-law about the plan, so they could leave and be safe. They thought he was joking and did not pay any attention to him. By morning, the angels were ready to begin their mission. They insisted Lot get himself and his family out of town immediately. Lot hesitated, and the angels needed to literally grab him, his wife, and his two daughters by the hand and rush them out of the city. The angels warned them to run into the mountains as fast as they could and not to look back. Then Lot began to argue! He convinced the angels that they couldn't possibly run that far, though they could make it to a small village nearby. The angels agreed to spare that small village for their protection, but that they could not wait any longer to leave. So Lot and his family ran. The city, along with several others in the plain, was destroyed by fire, which rained down on them from heaven. Lot and his family were spared, as the angels had promised. But Lot's wife did not listen to the warning and she looked back as they were running. She immediately turned into a pillar of salt.

At first, this seems a bit unfair. All she did was turn around and look. But, then, isn't that what causes us to lose faith as well? What do you think she was looking for? I would venture that she was concerned about her friends, her possessions, and the life she was leaving behind. Do you ever find yourself looking back in your life, wondering if things would be different if you had chosen a different path? The lesson for us in this story is that if we are following the path that God has set before us, as Lot and his wife were doing, then anything that we left behind is not something to be missed. God has wonderful things in store for us, and by feeling guilty about our choices, or longing for what we once had only stands in the way of our future. We show God a lack of trust when we doubt his plans for us. Doubt and guilt rob us of God's peace. God tells us, "Forget the former things; do not dwell on the past. See, I am doing a new thing! Now it springs up; do you not perceive it? I am making a way in the desert and streams in the wasteland" (Isaiah 43:18, 19, NIV).

So, we need to trust God to put us where He wants us, to give us what we need to do the work He gives us, and to be happy doing it. This is contentment, and this is peace. "Moreover, when God gives any man wealth and possessions, and enables him to enjoy them, to accept his lot and be happy is his work—this is a gift of God (Ecclesiastes 5:19, NIV). "Let your conduct be without covetousness; be content with such things as you have. For He Himself has said, 'I will never leave you nor forsake you' (Hebrews 13:5, NKJV). Solomon, in all his wisdom, wrote: "O God, I beg two favors from you before I die. First, help me never to tell a lie. Second, give me neither poverty nor riches! Give me just enough to satisfy my needs. For if I grow rich, I may deny you and say, "Who is the Lord?' And if I am too poor, I may steal and thus insult God's holy name" (Proverbs 30: 7-9, NLT). We must practice living in the present and being content with what God has blessed us with, and stop worrying about what we should have done and what may be coming next. We need to stop rushing around in a hurry to accomplish some future goal, while putting off our current happiness. We can still work toward a beautiful future; hard work and devotion are wonderful attributes, but we must keep in mind that while we are pushing ahead, great things are happening right now. Take the time to enjoy them. Thank God for the blessings he is showering down on you. Notice where you are in his plan for your life currently, and do what He is asking of you now. You have placed your life in God's hands, so stop worrying!

DON'T WORRY

The lord has promised to be with us as we travel along this road.
He tells us not to worry, for he will carry our load.
He asks us to share our sorrows, and our praises, too,
But letting go of all our troubles is a difficult thing to do.

Yes, god cares for the lilies and the sparrows and the land,
And he promises to care for us, to guide us with his hand.
We know that he is faithful, that his work is just and true,
Yet trying to handle it all on our own seems the natural thing to do.

"God helps those who help themselves" is what we've all been told.
Don't ask for help; that means you're weak. You must be strong and bold.
But Christ teaches us that this way of thinking is dead wrong.
The paradox is this: when we are weak, that's when we're strong.

The reality is that there is no power within us or without
That can change our lives, ease the struggles, and remove the doubt,
Except for Christ, who alone has power to do these things.
He alone is in control, as Lord of lords and King of kings.

So why would we want to deny ourselves the chance to be free,
By hanging on to our troubles, worrying about a future we cannot see.
God knows the end from the beginning and wants us to have peace.
Just trust him, let it go. Only then will your worries cease.

ATTITUDE OF GRATITUDE

Sometimes we find ourselves caught up in situations that are completely out of our control. We may be struck with a sudden illness or involved in an accident. Maybe some unexpected event has caught us off guard, like the car breaking down, or an unexpected bill showing up at the wrong time. We've all been there. It is often really difficult to understand why these things are happening.

And then there are the problems that we bring on ourselves. We face the consequences of choices that we make, or that others make that directly affect us. We get frustrated and anxious trying to figure out how to get ourselves out of these tight situations. The solutions aren't always simple or even apparent to us at times. We may feel like everything is spinning out of control, especially if we didn't cause the problem, we couldn't have prevented it, and we don't know where to turn to solve it. This is where trust in God becomes vital to our spiritual development.

We can trust that God will show us the solution and will not abandon us in our time of need. We can also focus our energy on what we can control, namely, our attitude. We always have a choice in how we respond to what is happening in our lives, even when we have no control over our circumstances.

Our attitude is a choice. We can react, out of anxiety and fear, or we can respond, out of love and trust in God.

One thing God wants from us during these times is an attitude of gratitude. The Bible says we should be thankful in all things. Colossians 1: 11, 12 tells us: "…May you be filed with joy, always thanking the Father, who has enabled you to share the inheritance that belongs to God's holy people, who live in the light" (NLT). We are told "Do not be anxious about anything, but in everything, by prayer and petition, with thanksgiving, present your requests to God. And the peace of God which transcends all understanding, will guard your hearts and your minds in Christ Jesus" (Philippians 4:6, 7, NIV). Here, God tells us plainly that one of the keys to having peace is presenting our requests with thanksgiving. We need to really focus on the blessings God has showered down on us. Thank Him for what we already have before we ask Him for what we think we still need.

We are even to keep our attitudes positive in the midst of our trials. Paul tells us in 2 Corinthians 7: 4, "…I am filled with comfort. I am exceedingly joyful in all our tribulation" (NKJV). He did not say he was pleased about his troubles, but that he remained joyful *in* his trouble. We can learn from this. We always have a choice to either accept what we are going through and remain positive, faithful people of God, with peace in our hearts, or to be anxious, unhappy, and fearful, not trusting in God to make "…all things work together for good to those who love God, to those who are the called according to His purpose" (Romans 8:28, NKJV).

I have battled for many years with depression. I had an exceptionally tough time with this when I became seriously ill. I had developed some abnormal uterine tissue growth which was causing me to bleed constantly. I had several biopsies done, but they were inconclusive, so I had no idea what may have been causing it. I was scared. I was also exhausted all the time from the chronic anemia, and I was having a lot of pain. Needless to say, I was more than a little grumpy. My negativity and lack of motivation to do much of anything rubbed off on others around me, straining my relationships at home and at work. This turned into a self-sustaining cycle: the depression made my relationships harder, which made me more frustrated and depressed.

I had surgery, which significantly improved my physical health, but for at least two months afterward, I still couldn't shake the depression. I felt completely helpless and out of control. I thought seriously about giving up. I started thinking up elaborate plans to end my life.

Through all of this, however, God did not abandon me. Even when I felt alone in this world and worthless, God continued to encourage me. As I spent much time in prayer and study of His word during this trial, I was able to understand what God wanted me to know. He reminded me of the many reasons I had to keep pressing on. He reminded me of the price that He paid to buy me back from the enemy, which helped me to appreciate my value to Him. He also helped me to see how my life was not really out of control. I learned that even when I felt I had no choice in what was happening, I still had choices in how I responded to the situations. He encouraged me to keep trusting Him, and He assured me that everything would be okay.

I knew that something had to change, so I decided to focus on myself. I followed God's promptings and made a conscious effort to adjust my attitude. I prayed earnestly for the strength to get emotionally well, and I used every opportunity to at least act happy. It took real effort some days, but it was not so hard at other times. I also consistently took time out every day to list all of the blessings I could think of and to thank God for them.

Over the next two to three months, I actually began to feel good. I realized that I really was thankful, and I really did feel blessed. The depression lifted, and I was able to compare how good I was feeling with how badly I had been feeling, and I couldn't help but be thankful for the change. My family and my coworkers noticed a difference, and my relationships began to improve. I also felt empowered to make some other positive changes in my life, because of the lessons I had learned about being able to control my attitude.

The scriptures give us clear direction on how to maintain this attitude of positive thinking. It is helpful to review them from time to time, perhaps even to commit them to memory. 1 Corinthians 15:58 states, "...be strong and steady, always enthusiastic about the Lord's work, for you know that nothing you do for the Lord is ever useless" (NLT). In referring to the Lord's work, this text is about everything we do, when done to God's glory. "So whether you eat or drink or whatever you do, do it all for the glory of God" (1 Corinthians 10:31, NIV). Imagine having the mindset that while you are driving to work on the freeway, you are driving to the glory of God. When you are at work, you are working to the glory of God. When you are taking out the trash, or cleaning your house, or cooking dinner, you are doing it all to the glory of God. God is with you in all of these seemingly mundane tasks, because you are doing them to his glory. Again, "And whatever you do, do it heartily, as to the Lord and not to men" (Colossians 3:23, NKJV). We can feel better about what we do when we keep in mind that we are doing it for God.

God tells us to protect our minds and to dwell on the good things in life, and this will strengthen our spirits. "Finally, brothers, whatever is true, whatever is noble, whatever is right, whatever is pure, whatever is lovely, whatever is admirable—if anything is excellent or praiseworthy—think about such things" (Philippians 4:8, NIV). "Set your minds on things above, not on earthly things" (Colossians 3:2, NIV). Paul tells Titus: "To the pure, everything is pure, but to those who are corrupted and do not believe, nothing is pure. In fact, both their minds and consciences are corrupted" (Titus 1:15, NIV). We are influenced by what we see and hear and what we think about. If we concentrate on pure, holy, loving thoughts, we will naturally become more pure, holy, and loving people. By keeping our thoughts fixed on Christ, we become more like Christ.

In contrast, the Bible warns us not to be anxious, complaining, worried people driven by fear. "And 'don't sin by letting anger gain control over you.' Don't let the sun go down while you are still angry, for anger gives a mighty foothold to the Devil" (Ephesians 4:26, 27, NLT). Paul tells us in Philippians 2:14, 15, "In everything you do, stay away from complaining and arguing, so that no one can speak a word of blame against you. You are to live clean, innocent lives as children of God in a dark world full of crooked and perverse people. Let your lives shine brightly before them" (NLT).

God expects us to be a light to our community. When people see us, they should see Christ in us. We are much more effective if we can thank God for His work, even in the midst of our trials, and remain upbeat and full of hope, rather than grumbling and reacting out of our anxiety. We must trust Him and allow His peace to fill our souls and banish the anxiety from our minds. Dwelling on God's blessings and having a persistent attitude of gratitude will take us far on our journey toward real peace.

Psalm 103:8, 9 tells us, "Let them give thanks to the Lord for his unfailing love and his wonderful deeds for men, for he satisfies the thirsty and fills the hungry with good things" (NIV). Thinking about our blessings, reminding ourselves that they all come from God, because He loves us, allows a character of gratitude to grow within us. We become more loving and more like Christ, and we become more conscious of God's ability to provide for us in our time of need. This helps our trust to grow and helps diminish our fears and anxieties. Colossians 3:15 states, "And let the peace that comes from Christ rule in your hearts. For as members of one body you are all called to live in peace. And always be thankful" (NLT).

One way of developing this thankful heart is through prayer. The Bible instructs us to "pray without ceasing" (1 Thessalonians 5:17, KJV). How do we do that? Not by kneeling at our bedside 24 hours a day, with head bowed and eyes closed, for sure. We are to always acknowledge God's concern for us, be aware of His presence, and talk to Him, thanking Him constantly. Imagine that God is sitting next to you as you drive to work. Think about Him as you make decisions, as you rejoice over good news or sorrow over losses. Ask Him to guide you. Talk to Him about what concerns you, as you would your best friend, which, by the way, He is! This is what He is asking for.

God says to us, "In those days when you pray, I will listen" (Jeremiah 29:12, NLT). God wants us to ask, to believe, and to trust in Him:

"If you need wisdom—if you want to know what God wants you to do— ask him, and he will gladly tell you. He will not resent your asking. But when you ask him, be sure that you really expect him to answer, for a doubtful mind is as unsettled as a wave of the sea that is driven and tossed by the wind. People like that should not expect to receive anything from the Lord. They can't make up their minds. They waver back and forth in everything they do" (James 1:5-8, NLT).

Does this sound familiar? I can certainly relate. I can count so many times that I have asked God to show me what I should do or where I should go. Then, when He answered me, I asked Him, "Are you sure? Was that really you, and was that really your answer?" I have struggled so much with doubt. But Christ says I can trust Him. He promises to hear my prayer and to answer, so why would I doubt that He would keep His word? He promises to give me what I need and to give me the power to do His will, so I have no reason to doubt, except for my fear or my selfishness, when the answer is not the easiest way out or the quickest solution.

Again, James tells us, "Confess your sins to each other and pray for each other so that you may be healed. The earnest prayer of a righteous person has great power and wonderful results" (James 5:16, NLT). Yes, prayer is one of the most powerful tools at our disposal. It keeps us connected to our source of strength. It is like plugging in to our power source.

Not only do we need to pray to God with our requests, but our conversations need to go both ways. We must also listen. I've heard it said that this is why we have two ears and only one mouth, so that we can listen twice as much as we speak! God tells us to "be still and know that I am God..." (Psalm 46:10, KJV). Satan loves to distract us with busyness, so that we cannot take the time to dwell on God's word or to listen to his "still small voice" (1 Kings 19:12, KJV). God does not demand our attention or yell out to us; rather, He waits for us to seek Him. Take the time to listen for His voice, to the soft murmurings of the Holy Spirit within you, directing your steps and guiding you into His presence. Look at God's creation, the life around you in plants, animals, mountains, deserts, oceans, and streams. Look up at the stars at night. Consider the mighty power of God to create the vastness of the universe, and yet have the compassion to care about your innermost secrets. David was in awe of this: "When I consider your heavens, the work of your fingers, the moon and the stars, which you have set in place, what is man that you are mindful of him, the son of man that you care for him?" (Psalm 8: 3, 4, NIV). God wants us to understand Him, through the things that He has given us.

In addition to prayer and meditation on God's blessings, we need to keep things in perspective. We tend to become so focused on our current problems and situations that we often fail to see "the big picture". 2 Corinthians 4:17, 18 tells us,

"For our present troubles are quite small and won't last very long. Yet they produce for us an immeasurably great glory that will last forever! So we don't look at the troubles we can see right now; rather, we look forward to what we have not yet seen. For the troubles we see will soon be over, but the joys to come will last forever" (NLT).

Imagine the peace we could have if we would realize that the things that keep us anxious are not as important as we often feel they are. What if we could relax a little more and trust God to work out the details? What if, when things turn out differently than we expect, we can tell ourselves that God must have something better in store for us, rather than feeling sorry for ourselves when things go wrong? What if we saw our trials and troubles as opportunities to grow or to reach out to someone else? Learning to see things from God's perspective is just another step on our journey to discover God's peace. Let's look at another example:

We pick up the story in Matthew 20. The owner of a vineyard went out one morning looking for men to hire for the day. "He agreed to pay the normal daily wage and sent them out to work" (v. 2, NLT). He went out four more times that day, finding men hanging around town with nothing else to do, "telling them he would pay them whatever was right at the end of the day" (v. 4).

"That evening he told the foreman to call the workers in and pay them, beginning with the last workers first. When those hired at five o'clock were paid, each received a full day's wage. When those hired earlier came to get their pay, they assumed they would receive more. But they, too, were paid a day's wage. When they received their pay, they protested, 'Those people worked only one hour, and yet you've paid them just as much as you paid us who worked all day in the scorching heat.'

"He answered one of them, 'Friend, I haven't been unfair! Didn't you agree to work all day for the usual wage? Take it and go. I wanted to pay this last worker the same as you. Is it against the law for me to do what I want with my money? Should you be angry because I am kind?" (Vv. 8-15).

Isn't that just like you and me? We think everything is going great until we start comparing ourselves with others around us. We appeal to our sense of fairness. We think we are being treated unfairly when someone else gets a break. These workers had agreed to an honest day's wages. They worked hard and got exactly what they had agreed upon and had expected. If they had not compared themselves to their coworkers, they would have been completely satisfied.

The landowner's response was precisely what they needed to hear. He did not cower from their accusations. He did not feel guilty. He just told them plainly that his business decisions were not their concern. Christ is like this. He treats us unfairly, by offering us grace instead of punishment. He gives us what we don't deserve, because he wants to, not because we have done anything to earn it. Life is not fair. We should remember how very, very fortunate we are that this is so! The next time we start to compare ourselves to someone else and feel that it is not fair that we are not as fortunate as our neighbor, we need to remember this story and be thankful that we serve a God who values mercy and grace enough to send His own son from heaven to take our penalty and offer us a gift we do not deserve. We can be grateful for the love that God offers us, as sinners, and rejoice in how unfair He can be, to step in and save us from the penalty that is rightfully ours! We can also know that it is never too late to accept his offer. Even at the last hour, the gift is exactly the same! Now that is something to be grateful for!

THE PARADOX

How can we feel so rushed and hurried,
On every matter vexed and worried,
When time can confine us for but a season?
Tomorrow promises eternity and joys beyond reason!

How can we sit perplexed and confused
Over changing values and opposing views,
When Your word is truth, and the way is clear?
Your wisdom is sound, for anyone that will hear.

How can we rely on our own strength and might
To control our own lives without seeking your light,
When only You know the end from the beginning,
And your plan is the one that ends with us winning?

How can we spend our hard-earned wages
On possessions and toys that become like cages,
Entrapping our souls on a quest for more gain,
When we could save for heaven, our work not in vain?

How can we give our enemy the power
To distract and confuse us hour by hour,
When we know your love and the joys we'll share
In heaven, once we join You there?

How can we be so slow to understand,
To see the touch of our Creator's hand,
When all around us the evidence is clear?
You are ever close, so very near.

PEACE IN GOD'S WORD

So, where do we go to find the solutions to life's problems, anyway? How do we find the answers we are looking for? We have studied a bit about presenting our requests to God in prayer, which is how we communicate our thoughts and desires to God. He then responds to us in His "still, small voice". But He also communicates to us in another, more tangible way, through His word. The Bible is like our instruction manual. It tells us who our maker is, what we were made for, and how to stay in working condition. It helps us to find direction for our lives and provides examples of how to do the work for which we were designed. It also gives us examples of what happens when we wander down the wrong road, which we are bound to do from time to time.

Personally, I am more thankful for the examples in the Bible of the "unsavory" characters that really seem to make a mess out of things than I am for the stories of the "saints". They give me hope that God can count me as a person of faith, just like he did David, Noah, Jacob, and Paul, to name a few. By showing us their mistakes and failures as well as their accomplishments and faithfulness, God demonstrates His love for us and give us hope of salvation, even though we are not perfect.

Besides providing examples and stories, God's word also provides us with advice and promises. It shows us the history of mankind and God's plans for our future. It leads us to an understanding of deep spiritual truths. It was given to us as a light to point us in the right direction: "Thy word is a lamp unto my feet, and a light unto my path" (Psalm 119:105, KJV). Hebrews tells us of the power of God's word: "For the word of God is full of living power. It is sharper than the sharpest knife, cutting deep into our innermost thoughts and desires. It exposes us for what we really are" (Hebrews 4:12, NLT). If God's word is this powerful, is it any wonder that Christ would tell us that we need it as much as food? "It is written: 'Man does not live on bread alone, but on every word that comes from the mouth of God'" (Matthew 4:4, NIV).

You may be thinking, "how can a book thousands of years old have any bearing on my life? Sure, it may have some neat stories and examples, but is it really relevant to me?" My answer is: absolutely! God's word is timeless. It is as relevant to you and I today as it was to Christ in His day. Jesus had only the Old Testament to work from, but He was able to teach the people about salvation from scriptures that were ancient even then. He was found in the synagogues, preaching from God's word regularly. Jesus told the religious leaders of His day, "You search the scriptures, for in them you think you have eternal life; and these are they which testify of me" (John 5:39, NKJV). Christ and his plan of redemption are found throughout the entire Bible. His love for us saturates His word. No matter where we read, we get glimpses of the character of God and His saving grace.

After His resurrection, Jesus met up with two of his disciples who were walking along the road from Jerusalem to Emmaus. They had just witnessed the brutal death of their Lord and were discussing the events, when Jesus came up to them, disguising himself, so they could not recognize Him, and asked them what they were talking about. They answered, "Are you the only stranger in Jerusalem, and have You not known the things which happened there in these days?" (Luke 24:18, NKJV). The disciples proceeded to fill the "stranger" in on the events of the preceding days, and how Christ's tomb was found empty. They expressed their fears and worries about what had happened and their uncertainty about their future. Then Jesus began to answer their unspoken questions and clarify the facts regarding His death and resurrection. "'O foolish ones, and slow of heart to believe in all that the prophets have spoken! Ought not the Christ to have suffered these things and to enter into His glory?' And beginning at Moses and all the Prophets, he expounded to them in all the Scriptures the things concerning Himself" (vv. 25-27). If, after His resurrection, Christ used the scriptures to show the disciples his truth, rather than to simply reveal Himself to them, then we must conclude that the scriptures were very valuable to Christ. And if the truth could be proven using only the Old Testament scriptures, then we must be very blessed, indeed, to have the New Testament to rely on as well!

Christ told his followers many, many times that the word of God was powerful. He used the Word as a defense against Satan by quoting scriptures every time Satan tempted Him in the wilderness. In fact, Christ not only *relied* on the word of God for guidance and for teaching, but He was *called* the Word of God. "In the beginning was the Word, and the Word was with God, and the Word was God" (John 1:1, NKJV). "And the Word became flesh and dwelt among us, and we beheld His glory, the glory as of the only begotten of the Father, full of grace and truth" (v. 14). Again, in Revelation 19:13, we are told, "He was clothed with a robe dipped in blood, and His name is called The Word of God" (NKJV). So, if the scriptures testify of Christ, and Christ even calls himself the Word of God, then reading the scriptures will definitely bring us into a deeper understanding of who Christ is. And as we begin to understand Him better, we will become more like Him. As we become more like Him, we will experience His peace.

As Christ was in the garden, praying, that last night before His death, He prayed fervently for His disciples and also for all believers that would ever follow Him. (That means you, and me!) He prayed, "Sanctify them by Your truth. Your word is truth" (John 17:17, NKJV). This means that we become sanctified, or made pure and holy, by God's word. God's word must be relevant to us, if it can make us holy. Peter describes the scriptures as, "…the word of God which lives and abides forever" and tells us"…the word of the lord endures forever" (1 Peter 1: 23, 25, NKJV). God's word is meant for us, today, just as much as it was meant for the disciples in Jesus' day. It had the power to change lives then, and it continues to do the same today. God speaks to us every time we pick up His word and listen to what He says.

That is exactly how this book came about. I was going through some very difficult struggles in my life. I have a problem with control. I am quite happy when everything is going smoothly in my life. I can even accept it when things go wrong, as long as I can do something to change my circumstances and make things right again. But when things are out of my control, and there is nothing I can do about it, I have a real hard time accepting it.

This is an area where God has had to work on me a lot. I get "stressed out" easily, and I need to learn to trust God more and worry less. At one particular point, when I was feeling overwhelmed and under a great deal of stress, I asked myself, "How can I stop feeling like this and, instead, take hold of the peace that God offers me?"

I began to study the scriptures to find the answer to that question, and the result is this book. I studied, prayed, and meditated on the thoughts God presented to me. I wrote them in a journal and began to incorporate them into my daily life, and, amazingly, it worked! I really began to feel less stressed and less out of control, even though my circumstances had not changed. I realized that even if I could not control each and every detail of my life, I could control my attitude, and I could trust God to control the rest. In studying the scriptures, I found the answer I was looking for.

Studying God's word can bless us in many ways. "All scripture is God-breathed and is useful for teaching, rebuking, correcting and training in righteousness, so that the man of God may be thoroughly equipped for every good work" (2 Timothy 3:16, 17, NIV). It teaches us, through God's law, through history, through stories and parables, and through examples. It rebukes us by revealing our sins, so that we can take appropriate action: "...it was the law that showed me my sin. I would never have known that coveting is wrong if the law had not said, 'Do not covet.'" (Romans 7:7, NLT). It corrects us, by showing us God's grace and forgiveness, so that we can try again and learn from our mistakes. It trains us by teaching us God's ideal plan for our lives and showing us how to follow Him.

The Bible is our answer book. It tells us what to do and how to live. Amos 3:7 tells us, "Surely the Sovereign Lord does nothing without revealing his plan to his servants the prophets" (NIV). He shares with us His overall plans for the universe. He tells us what to expect in the future. He reveals to us the big picture, so we won't be surprised as events unfold. But He also shares His plans for us, individually, as we seek to discover His will for our own lives in His word.

God promises to bless us as we seek Him for our answers:

> " 'For I know the plans I have for you,' declares the Lord, 'plans to prosper you and not to harm you, plans to give you hope and a future. Then you will call upon me and come and pray to me, and I will listen to you. You will seek me and find me when you seek me with all your heart'" (Jeremiah 29: 11-13, NIV).

We can search for God and we can find Him in His word. The Bible speaks of this searching of God's word for truth: "Now the Bereans were of more noble character than the Thessalonians, for they received the message with great eagerness and examined the scriptures every day to see if what Paul said was true" (Acts 17:11, NIV). God wants us to search for him, to ask Him questions, to try to understand him. He delights in our quest to know him better and to receive His blessings. After all, what father wouldn't want his children to spend time with him and get to know him better? God gives us everything we need in his word, and it is there for the asking. All we have to do is pick it up and read it for ourselves.

So, how do we get started in studying God's word? How do we get the answers we are looking for? There are as many techniques to studying God's word as there are people to study it. You can read it cover to cover. You can get a chart that organizes the scriptures to help you to read through the entire Bible in a year. You can open it randomly and start reading wherever the spirit leads you. You can use a concordance and look up every scripture under a specific category. The choices are endless. However you choose to begin, you will be blessed. The only advice I would offer is to be sure to pray for guidance from the Holy Spirit each time you open your Bible and begin to read, so that you will have a blessing and gain understanding. Beyond that, there is no right or wrong way to read God's word and learn about Him.

Of course, my favorite part of studying God's word is finding all of the powerful promises that He gives us to assure us of His presence in our lives. "Your promise revives me; it comforts me in all my troubles" (Psalm 119:50, NLT). God promises to care for all of our needs: "Humble yourselves, therefore, under God's mighty hand, that he may lift you up in due time. Cast all your anxiety on him because he cares for you" (1 Peter 5:6, 7, NIV). What a comfort to know that the God of the vast universe cares for us, individually, and is concerned about our needs. "Therefore I tell you, whatever you ask for in prayer, believe that you have received it, and it will be yours" Jesus tells us (Mark 11:24, NIV). God is simply waiting for us to ask!

He also promises to protect us in our times of trial: "If the Lord delights in a man's way, he makes his steps firm; though he stumble, he will not fall, for the Lord upholds him with his hand" (Psalm 37: 23, 24, NIV). Can't you just picture that for a moment: you are walking along the path of life, with God's hand firmly holding yours, so you cannot fall? What a wonderful, caring God we serve! Again, the Bible assures us:

"But remember that the temptations that come into your life are no different from what others experience. And God is faithful. He will keep the temptation from becoming so strong that you can't stand up against it. When you are tempted, he will show you a way out so that you will not give in to it" (1 Corinthians 10:13, NLT).

God is always there to help direct us in every decision we are faced with, if we only stop to seek His guidance. He also promises to give us the strength and power to carry out the plan He has laid out for us. "And the God of all grace, who called you to his eternal glory in Christ, after you have suffered a little while, will himself restore you and make you strong, firm, and steadfast" (1 Peter 5:10, NIV). I rely on this verse to get me through many of my struggles. I depend on God to make me steadfast and strong. What a comfort to know that His plans are to restore me and to call me to His eternal glory!

Another verse, which I would recommend you commit to memory, to serve you in times of anxiety, is: "I can do all things through Christ who strengthens me" (Philippians 4:13, NKJV). And one of my favorite verses regarding the power of God's love in our lives is this:

"And I pray that Christ will be more and more at home in our hearts as you trust in him. May your roots go down deep into the soil of God's marvelous love. And may you have the power to understand, as all

God's people should, how wide, how long, how high, and how deep his love really is. May you experience the love of Christ, though it is so great you will never fully understand it. Then you will be filled with the fullness of life and power that comes from God" (Ephesians 3:17-19, NLT).

We will never fully understand God's love, but we can accept and appreciate it. It is real, it is ours, and it is limitless!

Another favorite that I wish to share is: "For God has not given us a spirit of fear and timidity, but of power, love, and self-discipline" (2 Timothy 1:7, NLT). I have always found it helpful to remember what God has given me and how God has equipped me when I have difficult decisions to make or obstacles to overcome. God gave us our character and all of our strengths. We can draw daily from God's word the strength that we need to tackle any challenge that we may face.

Not only does God promise us his protection, strength, and power, but He also promises us a future with Him in heaven and a chance to grow and develop our characters throughout our lives here on earth. I can't begin to count the texts that refer to our new life after this one, but I would like to point out a couple of verses that can help us in our struggles while we are here: "I will give you a new heart and put a new spirit in you; I will remove from you your heart of stone and give you a heart of flesh" (Ezekiel 36:26, NIV) and, "…I am sure that God, who began the good work within you, will continue his work until it is finally finished on that day when Christ Jesus comes back again" (Philippians 1:6, NLT). God never stops working on us, helping us to become all that He has in store for us. He gives us everything that is at his disposal to encourage us, lift us up, and strengthen us to do His work.

I encourage you to search God's word for yourself, to find God's blessings and His peace through His message, which was written for you. God promises to bless you through his word: "…so is my word that goes out from my mouth: It will not return to me empty, but will accomplish what I desire and achieve the purpose for which I sent it" (Isaiah 55:11, NIV). Trust Him to lead you. Read His word, memorize it, and meditate on it. You will not be disappointed!

SPIRITUAL WARFARE

Being the goal-directed, anxiety-ridden, control-seeking, type-A, overachiever that I am, I must confess that understanding, and even more, attaining a spirit of peace within my soul has been a real struggle for me. I have to ask God daily for guidance and strength in this area. All too often, I find myself feeling guilty about not having it all together and acting like I think a "real" Christian should act. There are times when I think I have it all figured out, only to fall flat on my face the moment the next struggle comes my way. I feel like Paul, when he says in Romans 7: 15: "I don't understand myself at all, for I really want to do what is right, but I don't to it. Instead, I do the very thing I hate" (NLT). Again, in verse 19: "When I want to do good, I don't. And when I try not to do wrong, I do it anyway."

I experience this every day, as I try to make the right decisions, in this world where things don't always make sense, and the right choices aren't always obvious. I am consistently bombarded with conflicting information from all directions. As a Christian, I tend to hold myself to a higher standard than I expect of my friends and neighbors. After all, Jesus is my role model, and He was perfect, so shouldn't I expect to be perfect, too? As I keep striving to reach such a lofty goal, I become aware of how far short of the mark I actually come. This creates quite a struggle within my heart.

This often leads me to question my faith and commitment to God. I tend to think that if I truly trusted God and followed His leading in my life, then I wouldn't have such a conflict within my soul. But this is not the case in our walk with God. He doesn't promise any of us the easy life. "...narrow is the gate and difficult is the way which leads to life, and there are few who find it" (Matthew 7:14, NKJV). Life is hard, and we usually don't get to take the easy way out.

We have already discussed how God uses trials to help build our characters, but I believe there is much more to it than this. What we often fail to recognize is that we are in the midst of a cosmic conflict, a war, if you will, between Christ and Satan, between good and evil. The battlefield is right here, on planet earth, on our own soil, and in our own hearts and minds. It is a battle in which our very salvation, our eternal life, is at stake, so we need to be acutely aware of what is happening. This battle began millennia ago, in heaven, not on earth:

"And there was war in heaven. Michael and his angels fought against the dragon, and the dragon and his angels fought back. But he was not strong enough, and they lost their place in heaven. The great dragon was hurled down—that ancient serpent called the devil, or Satan, who leads the whole world astray. He was hurled to the earth, and his angels with him" (Revelation 12:7-9, NIV).

We don't usually think of heaven as a place of war. But it happened. And since Satan and his angels were cast out of heaven and sent here to earth, we are now living right in the middle of the battlefield! And we are not the only ones involved. Our choices affect others, "...we have been made a spectacle to the whole universe, to angels as well as to men" (1 Corinthians 4:9, NIV). This is not just a small skirmish, but a full-on war, with eternal consequences.

This certainly helps to explain the battle that wages inside each of us. Our enemy is diligent in his duty, to turn us from Christ. "Be careful! Watch out for attacks from the Devil, your great enemy. He prowls around like a roaring lion, looking for some victim to devour" (1 Peter 5:8, NLT). "For we are not fighting against people made of flesh and blood, but against the evil rulers and authorities of the unseen world, against those mighty powers of darkness who rule this world, and against wicked spirits in the heavenly realms" (Ephesians 6:12, NLT). This is serious! Satan is actively seeking to destroy us. Thankfully, we have nothing to fear! God provides us with everything we need to fight this battle. Continuing on in Ephesians chapter six, we read about the armor that God provides us, to shield us from the weapons of the devil:

"Stand your ground, putting on the sturdy belt of truth and the body armor of God's righteousness. For shoes, put on the peace that comes from the Good News, so that you will be fully prepared. In every battle you will need faith as your shield to stop the fiery arrows aimed at you by Satan. Put on salvation as you helmet, and take the sword of the Spirit, which is the word of God. Pray at all times and on every occasion in the power of the Holy Spirit. Stay alert and be persistent in your prayers for all Christians everywhere" (vv. 14-18, NLT).

Each piece of this armor is a specific weapon that God gives us, to protect us from our enemy. Please notice that the shoes are shoes of peace. The very peace that we are seeking is a piece of His armor! Since shoes are for the protection of our feet, and we use our feet to get around, then with your feet shod with His peace, you can go anywhere He needs you to go!

I have often visualized myself putting on this armor, when facing a difficult challenge. I carefully reflect on each item, as I imagine myself dressing for battle. It helps me to concentrate on God's protection in the midst of this spiritual battle. When I see the big picture, it helps me to make the right decisions, even when they are tough to make.

So, what about our enemy? How can we recognize him? Is he really a creature in a red suit with a pitchfork in his hand and a pointy tail? The Bible describes him this way: "And no wonder! For Satan himself transforms himself into an angel of light" (2 Corinthians 11: 14, NKJV). Of course he would appear as an angel. Who would pay any attention to him at all if we could recognize him and see him as he truly is? He deceives us. "...He was a murderer from the beginning, and does not stand in the truth, because there is no truth in him. When he speaks a lie, he speaks from his own resources, for he is a liar and the father of it" (John 8:44, NKJV). But we don't have to be deceived.

God promises us throughout His word that He will protect us. "He will shield you with his wings. He will shelter you with his feathers. His faithful promises are your armor and protections" (Psalms 91:4, NLT). Did you catch that? His promises are our armor. That is just one more reason to study His word. Again, He tells us:

"No, in all these things we are more than conquerors through him who loved us. For I am convinced that neither death nor life, neither angels nor demons, neither the present nor the future, nor any powers, neither height nor depth, nor anything else in all creation, will be able to separate us from the love of God that is in Christ Jesus our Lord" (Romans 8:37-39, NIV).

There is nothing that is powerful enough to separate us from God's love. Nothing! Just knowing that fills my heart with peace. That peace can be yours, too, because Isaiah the prophet wrote, "You will keep him in perfect peace, whose mind is stayed on You, because he trusts in You" (Isaiah 26:3, NKJV).

Furthermore, we are told, "Behold, I give you the authority to trample on serpents and scorpions, and over all the power of the enemy, and nothing shall by any means hurt you" (Luke 10:19, NKJV). God gives us amazing power! No one really has any power over us that we don't allow them to have, because God gives us power over our enemies. That means my boss, my spouse, my children, or my neighbors cannot take away the peace that God gives me, unless I let them. They may hurt me by firing me, taking away my privileges, or hurting me some other way, but they cannot really hurt me, for they cannot take away anything that God gives me. God is bigger than our enemies, and he gives us access to His power over them as well.

Again, "So, if you are suffering according to God's will, keep on doing what is right, and trust yourself to the God who made you, for he will never fail you" (1 Peter 4:19, NLT). This one has helped me when I have questioned my decisions. I am certain that if I am doing what is right, God is on my side, no matter who may be upset with my choices. As a nurse, I sometimes have to make choices in my patients' best interest that may not make everyone happy. I have to remember that if I choose to do what is right, then it doesn't matter who may be offended. I have God's blessing, and that is what counts.

Another amazing verse tells us, "Submit yourselves, then, to God. Resist the devil, and he will flee from you," (James 4:7, NIV). Again, we have an example of the power that God gives us in this battle of good versus evil. Moreover, "We are hard pressed on every side, but not crushed; perplexed, but not in despair; persecuted, but not abandoned; struck down, but not destroyed" (2 Corinthians 4: 8, 9, NIV). Now, this is peace! This is exactly the attitude we need to have at all times, in all circumstances. No matter what, God will not fail us. The Bible is full of such promises.

The most important thing to keep in mind is that this is really not our battle. It is God's. And since it is His battle, He is willing and able to give us everything we need to win it. David knew this when he battled against Goliath. How else could he fight a giant, without armor and armed with only a slingshot? He knew that God would give him the victory, because Goliath was not only opposing Israel, but God himself. God would win the battle for himself, if David would only stand up against the giant. You can read this in 1 Samuel chapter 18.

In another story, the prophet Jahaziel said the same thing, as he assured King Jehoshaphat and all of Israel, "…This is what the Lord says to you: 'Do not be afraid or discouraged because of this vast army. For the battle is not yours, but God's…" (2 Chronicles 20:15, NIV). God knows that our battle here on earth is really His battle. He is with us through it all and will give us strength and guidance to win the victory.

The Bible is full of examples of God intervening in miraculous ways to give victory to his people in times of overwhelming odds. One such example is found in 2 Kings, chapter 6. The nation of Israel was at war with Aram. It was the prophet, Elisha's, duty to warn the king of Israel about when and where the king of Aram was planning his next attack. God was clearly present with the Israelites, and He was protecting them. The king of Aram became very angry that his plans kept getting spoiled, and he was sure there was a traitor in his camp. One of the officers alerted the king that "Elisha, the prophet in Israel, tells the king of Israel even the words you speak in the privacy of your bedroom" (v. 12, NLT). The king immediately called for the capture of Elisha. The army of Aram surrounded the city where Elisha was staying. When Elisha's servant woke up in the morning, he saw the enemy army with all of its horses and chariots surrounding the city, and he asked Elisha what they should do.

Elisha replied, "Don't be afraid…For there are more on our side than on theirs!" (v. 16). Then Elisha prayed for the Lord to open the servant's eyes, so he could see what was happening behind the scenes. "The Lord opened his servant's eyes, and when he looked up, he saw that the hillside around Elisha was filled with horses and chariots of fire" (v.17). Imagine the peace we would have if we were aware of the unseen armies that protect us! We would never fear! God's word assures us that what we can see is not all that there is. Psalms 91: 11-13, tells us, "For he orders his angels to protect you wherever you go. They will hold you with their hands to keep you from striking your foot on a stone. You will trample down lions and poisonous snakes; you will crush fierce lions and serpents under your feet!" (NLT). What an amazing promise! And we can trust that it is true, because God said it.

God also tells us, "…he who began a good work in you will carry it on to completion until the day of Christ Jesus" (Philippians 1:6, NIV). God started it, and He promises to finish it. And He has the power to do it. Our job is only to trust Him. We must have the faith to allow Him to carry out His purposes in our lives. He promises to give us the strength to persevere and to reward us for our faithfulness: "Blessed is the man who perseveres under trial, because when he has stood the test, he will receive the crown of life that God has promised to those who love him" (James 1:12, NIV).

This particular text has been a profound blessing to me. I went to college when my children were toddlers. At the same time, my first husband was in and out of jail and was not providing financially or emotionally to our family. When he was home, he was abusive. Most of the time, though, I was alone. I carried a heavy load of what I called "mother guilt," as I was not able to devote the amount of quality time to my children that I had hoped I could. I definitely felt like I was under trial. I remember sitting on my bed with my books spread open and sobbing because I couldn't see how I was going to make it.

I kept this verse posted on my refrigerator, and I read it over and over again. It was a constant reminder to me that God would see me through this difficult time, and that it would all be worth it in the end. God's promises provided me with the strength I needed to keep pressing on, no matter how hard it was.

Christ has promised us this blessing as well: "I have told you all this so that you may have peace in me. Here on earth you will have many trials and sorrows. But take heart, because I have overcome the world" (John 16:33, NLT). This sums it up, doesn't it? We can have peace because Christ has already won! He has overcome! Through Him, we also will overcome and have the promise to become heirs with Him in His kingdom. We may struggle through battles, but the victory is already ours, because Christ has won, and we are His! This assurance is our true source of peace. All we need to do is accept it and it is ours.

It is my fervent prayer for you that you will allow the Holy Spirit to work in you and that you will listen to God speak to your heart and will open yourself up to His peace. I hope that you will learn to trust Him in all things and be assured of your personal victory in your own battles. And I pray that you will not become discouraged when the battles seem tough. Remember that God has already won, and that your reward is waiting for you just around the corner. "And behold, I am coming quickly, and my reward is with Me, to give to every one according to his work" (Revelation 22:12, NKJV). Keep your eyes on Christ and he will give you the peace you seek.

MY PRAYER

Here I am again, Lord,
Down on my knees in prayer.
I've blown it once again, Lord;
My heart is filled with despair.

I try to make it on my own,
Struggling in my own power.
I feel so desperate and alone.
I need you hour by hour.

The world around me seems so cruel.
My enemy knows me well!
He uses against me every tool.
My failures he loves to tell!

The darkness locks me in so tight;
I feel there is no way out,
But I know I'm still within your sight,
So why am I so filled with doubt?

I long for the day I'll be set free
From this world of sorrow and sin,
But your grace is sufficient for me,
So I guess I can try once again.

I lay my burdens down at your feet.
I will trust in your mercy and grace.
My enemy runs away in defeat,
As you help me to win this race.

You never promised me an easy life.
In fact, you promised me trials.
I learn so much in my constant strife,
As I wander these weary miles.

But through all the trouble and the pain,
You are always right by my side.

Spiritual Warfare

With all the treasures of heaven to gain,
In your loving arms I can safely hide.

Thank you for filling me with your peace
To replace all the fear and the pain.
My burden, now, I will gladly release
And trust you to heal me once again.

Appendix 1: Discussion Questions

Chapter 1: We are Called to Forgive

1.) Think of the most recent conflict you have had with a friend or relative. How could patience have helped to resolve the conflict and prevent angry, hurt feelings?

2.) What destructive methods might you be using to cope with deep frustrations, hidden anger, or unresolved conflict? How might discussing these openly with God in prayer help you to begin healing?

3.) What barriers are you facing that may be keeping you from offering your whole heart to God?

4.) Thinking about the story of the prodigal son, do you relate more to the lost son or to the other son or both? Why?

5.) How can thinking about how much God has forgiven you help you to be more forgiving toward others?

Chapter 2: Forgiving our Enemies

1.) Is there anyone in your past that has hurt you to a point that you feel you cannot forgive them? What is keeping you from making the first step and asking for God's help?

2.) What does the scripture in Romans 12:17-21 mean to you, when it advises being kind to your enemies, and that in so doing "you will heap burning coals on his head?" Is God asking us to be kind as a form of revenge? Explain your answer.

3.) What are you doing in your life to show God that you are willing to follow Him, even when you do not know all of the details?

4.) How can understanding that our response to others can have eternal consequences help us in being more forgiving?

5.) Knowing that Christ has been tempted just as you are, what could be keeping you from trusting Him completely?

Chapter 3: Forgiving and Forgetting

1.) Have you been holding back and refusing to forgive someone, because you know you could never forget what happened? Does it help to know that forgetting is not a condition of forgiveness?

2.) How does your memory strengthen your hope in God's saving grace? Give an example.

3.) How does God's willingness to forgive our sins and never recall them testify to the whole universe about his character?

4.) Imagine what the world would be like if we were like God, delighting in showing mercy. How can you make this change in your own life?

5.) In what way has the enemy tried to convince you that God has not completely forgiven your sins?

6.) How is guilt robbing you of God's peace right now?

Chapter 4: What Peace is Not

1.) Give an example of how God has used trials and conflicts to develop your character.

2.) Think about what lessons Jesus may have learned through suffering. How does that help you to understand that God knows your own pain?

3.) Think of a time that you felt completely overwhelmed, like Paul, and could see no way out of a situation. What did God do that shows you that you can trust him?

4.) Do you find comfort in the stories of God's faithful servants that have made mistakes just like you do? How can this help you in your own walk with God?

Chapter 5: What is Peace?

1.) Define peace in your own words.

2.) Give an example of what you can do to make your heart more open to God's counsel.

3.) How does Christ's sacrifice for you assure you during your trials?

4.) Think of the young men's response to the king in the story of the fiery furnace. How can trusting in God's ability to save you, both immediately and eternally, help you to overcome anxiety and help you not to worry?

5.) When you are overwhelmed, does it help you to look at "the big picture" and consider the overall scope of your problem? Explain.

Chapter 6: A Sabbath Rest

1.) In what way have you devoted special time to developing your relationship with God?

2.) What things in your life that may be competing with your ability to spend time with God?

3.) In what ways are your relationships suffering from neglect? What steps can you take to rekindle them?

4.) Think of a way that you can spend time doing something good on the Sabbath. How can you use this time to strengthen your relationship with God and be a blessing to others?

Chapter 7: Contentment

1.) How do you know when God is prompting you to make a certain decision? What specific methods does he use most effectively with you?

2.) Examine your current goals. What will it take for you to be satisfied with your life?

3.) Do you relate to Paul, who is content with having everything or with having nothing? Why or why not?

4.) Have you ever experienced a time when God seemed to be ignoring your pain or refusing to answer your prayers? How did you cope with this feeling?

5.) What is keeping you from being content right now?

6.) When Paul states, "when I am weak, then I am strong," what does that mean to you?

7.) Is there anything that is calling you to look back as Lot's wife did? Explain how you can learn from this story and move forward without regret.

Chapter 8: Attitude of Gratitude

1.) How can you stay positive in the midst of a difficult trial? Give some specific examples.

2.) How does thinking of everything you do as something done to God's glory help you to have peace?

3.) How would y our life be different if you only did those things which were noble, right, pure, lovely, and admirable?

4.) List 10 things that your are thankful for right now.

5.) How might doubt be keeping you from trusting God?

Chapter 9: Peace in God's Word

1.) What problems are you facing that you have not searched God's word to help you answer?

2.) How does it help you to know that God has a plan for your life?

3.) What can we learn about God's love for us by reading the promises in His word?

4.) How does it make you feel to know that God will never stop working on you, preparing your heart for eternity?

5.) How can you improve your study habits and spend more time learning about God's love through his word?

Chapter 10: Spiritual Warfare

1.) Do you ever get discouraged, feeling that you aren't good enough for God? Give an example.

2.) How does our understanding of our role in a great battle help us to defeat temptation?

3.) Is there anything that you have thought could separate you from God's love? How does knowing that no power, not even death, can do that help strengthen your faith?

4.) Does God's promise that He will never fail you if you do His will give you strength to stand up for what is right?

5.) How does it help you to know that the battle is really God's and not ours? Give examples of how this thinking can help you in your own struggles.

6.) How do you feel, knowing you are on the winning team?

Printed in the United States
50907LVS00003B/158

April 7, 2019
Judas
Series: Villains
Pastor KenMcIntyre

This series examines notorious people involved with the crucifixion and death of Jesus. We will see the tensions and struggles they faced and how they reflect us.

Judas' background:
- Judas was one of the 12 disciples of Jesus. Judas made a deep commitment to Jesus, and there's no reason to think Judas was anything but sincere in his faith. Like the rest of the disciples, Judas thought Jesus was of such extraordinary value that he left everything to follow Him.
- Unlike the rest of the disciples, Judas was the only one not from the region of Galilee. Judas often goes by the title "Judas Iscariot". "Iscariot" means "Man of Kerioth". Kerioth was a town in south Judea. Judeans prided themselves on being pure-blooded Jews and looked on Galilee with contempt because there were a lot of non-Jews (Gentiles) in that area. On top of that, Galileans were often poor and uneducated.
- Judas was more cultured. He was well spoken; he was from a better place with a better reputation.
- Judas was trusted by Jesus and the disciples because he was in charge of the money.

Judas' understanding of "Messiah"
- Most Bible scholars tell us that Judas had an Old Testament understanding of who the Messiah was going to be, and what the Messiah was going to do.
- "Messiah" means 'promised deliverer'.
- Judas understood that the Messiah was going to be a military or political leader. At this point in history, Rome has invaded and conquered Israel. Judas would've understood the Messiah to be someone who would be able to deliver Israel from Roman rule and return Israel to independence.
- Jesus acted like the Messiah Judas was hoping for in many ways (ex. Jesus healed the sick/blind/lame, raised the dead, preached the Gospel to the poor).

- But other times, Jesus did not act like the Messiah Judas wanted (ex. Jesus didn't hate the Romans, Jesus was at odds with the temple leaders, Jesus didn't seem concerned about money which was required to overthrow the Romans).
- Jesus didn't behave the way Judas expected Jesus to behave, and so Judas didn't behave the way he ought to (see Matthew 26:6 – Matthew 27:5)

The Trade
- Judas traded Jesus for 30 pieces of silver (the price of a slave in the 1st century). What was of extraordinary value in one moment, had no value in the next.
- How could Judas go so wrong? Because Judas relationship with Jesus was built on a bargain style arrangement (*If you will, then I will*).
- When Judas realizes that Jesus will be condemned to die, Judas "*was seized with remorse and returned the thirty pieces of silver*" (Matthew 27:3)
- In that sense, we can be a lot like Judas. Every time we sin, we are making a trade. We are trading what we wanted Jesus to do or to be for us, with something else only to realize that it wasn't worth it.
- The story of Judas reminds us that nothing good can come from trading in Jesus.

"I will, even if you won't"
- The *"If you will, then I will"* bargain style of faith doesn't work. It will destroy your relationship with God. What do you do, when you can't manipulate God?
- Look to the cross. You end up seeing a love without any conditions. You don't see an *"if you will, then I will"* situation. Instead, you see an *"I will, even if you don't"* situation.
- God doesn't need you to love him, in order for him to love you.
- But his love for you demonstrated on the cross compels us to love Him in return.
- When we're able to surrender our lives to God's love, we're not tempted to manipulate God to our own benefit. We realize the benefit itself is knowing and being known by Jesus.
- A relationship with God isn't something to be leveraged or controlled, but to be enjoyed because Jesus is of extraordinary worth. Don't trade it for anything.